REMEMBERING
AYRTON SENNA

REMEMBERING
AYRTON SENNA

Alan Henry
Photography by John Townsend

Motorbooks International
Publishers & Wholesalers ®

Contents

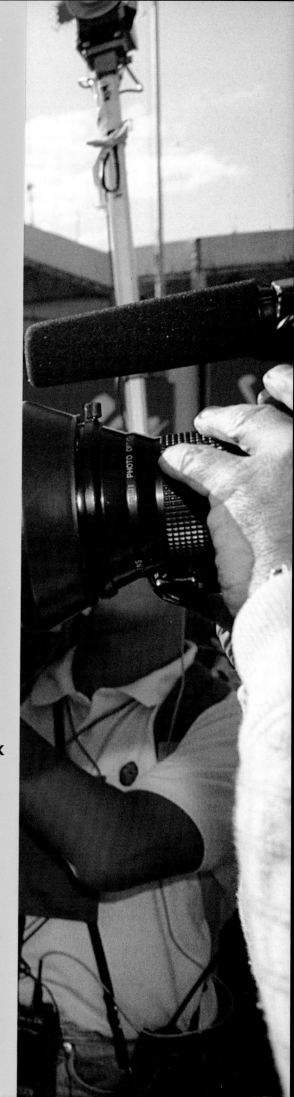

1

THE DEATH OF A STAR

After disappointing performances in the first two rounds of the 1994 title chase Ayrton Senna had predicted "the real battle for the World Championship begins at Imola." Yet the San Marino Grand Prix was destined to be the most tragic motor race in a generation. The brilliant Brazilian was snatched from the Formula One stage at the peak of his career. Grand Prix racing had lost its leader.

(Preceding pages)
Grim faces all
round as the
Grand Prix drivers
congregate on the
starting grid at
Monaco to pay
tribute to their
fallen comrade.

In the flickering half-light of dawn Varig Airlines Flight RG723 from Paris to São Paulo clicked off the final few miles of its seemingly endless journey across the Atlantic Ocean and finally entered Brazilian airspace. It was Wednesday, 4 May 1994. Captain Gomes Pinto had flown the route many times before, but this was a flight like no other in his career.

As he gradually eased the McDonnell Douglas MD-11 down from its cruising altitude of 35,000

millionaire international sportsman and a man adored to the point of deification in his native land. It was a journey he had made countless times before, either by commercial airliner or, more recently, in his own immaculate $12 million British Aerospace executive jet.

Ayrton Senna was returning to São Paulo to a state funeral the like of which few people in that bustling metropolis could ever remember. Brazil was a nation in mourning for a man who had given it

In the Williams–Renault FW16 during the last race of his life, the fateful 1994 San Marino Grand Prix at Imola. That he started from pole position as fastest qualifier was a triumph of his brilliance over the difficult-to-drive machine.

feet for the final run into São Paulo's Guarulos international airport, a posse of Brazilian air-force jets took up station on either side of the giant aircraft. Yet this was no moment of high drama. It was a gesture of supreme respect for one of their country's greatest national heroes, who was coming home for the last time. Captain Pinto later described the flight as the saddest of his life. "Every time we passed another plane, they offered their condolences over the radio," he said.

Flight RG723 was carrying the body of Ayrton Senna da Silva – Grand Prix motor-racing champion,

self-respect and esteem through his exploits on motor-racing circuits around the globe.

His death in the San Marino Grand Prix at Imola four days earlier had rocked the world of motor racing to its very foundations. The thirty-four-year-old Brazilian had been leading the fourth round of the 1994 World Championship at the wheel of his Williams–Renault, ahead of his formidable young rival Michael Schumacher's Benetton–Ford, when he unaccountably speared off the circuit on the flat-out Tamburello left-hander just beyond the pits at the Autodromo Enzo e Dino Ferrari.

Senna lost control, whether through driver error or mechanical failure, at just over 190 mph. In the eighteen metres from the point his Williams deviated from the prescribed racing line, which it covered in barely a second, he managed to slow the car to around 135 mph before hitting the vertical concrete retaining wall on the right-hand side of the circuit.

The right front wheel of the Williams was ripped off in the huge impact, and the car catapulted back towards the edge of the track, scattering mechanical debris in all directions. Travelling at 190 mph, Schumacher was past the accident site almost before the moment of impact, but the next car on the scene was the third-placed Ferrari driven by Austria's Gerhard Berger – a close friend and former team-mate of Senna's.

Berger barely had a moment to take in what was happening before he, too, was past the scene. By then the race officials had absorbed the enormity of the accident and red-flagged the race to a halt; by then Berger had completed another half-lap at racing speed. When he eventually climbed from the cockpit, he shuddered to see that his car's front suspension remained attached to the chassis by a thin strand of metal, almost severed by debris from Senna's car which was now firmly wedged beneath his Ferrari.

At the accident scene Senna was clearly grievously injured. The circuit's medical helicopter was despatched to land in the middle of the track, and the injured driver was immediately flown to Bologna's Maggiore hospital for specialist attention. At 6:40 that same evening Ayrton Senna was pronounced dead.

By that time the race had been restarted, re-run and produced a commanding victory for Schumacher. Despite having no stomach for the job, Berger had taken the restart, briefly leading before being overtaken by Schumacher. Berger then came into the pits, convinced that something was wrong with the rear end of his car. Subsequently it was discovered that the Ferrari had a faulty rear shock-absorber, but Gerhard had already quietly retired. He was

(Above) After seeing him for six seasons at the wheel of a red-and-white Marlboro McLaren, the F1 community found it difficult to become accustomed to the sight of Senna's bright yellow helmet in the cockpit of the Williams–Renault, here seen in action at Imola 1994. (Below) The way we remember him. A rear shot of the Williams–Renault FW16 during practice for the 1994 San Marino Grand Prix, Senna's head tilted slightly to the right as he scans his rear-view mirror for sight of the opposition.

After the startline collision at Imola the field circulated for several laps behind the safety car while marshals cleared debris from the circuit. Here Senna's Williams leads the pack at reduced speed before the restart.

confused, distressed and fully appreciated the extent of Senna's accident even before the final mind-numbing news filtered back to the circuit.

The Grand Prix fraternity was already in a state of shock following the death of Austrian novice Roland Ratzenberger after a crash in the previous afternoon's second qualifying session. The pleasant young man from Salzburg had been the first person to die at the wheel of a Formula One car for almost a decade. Standards of Grand Prix car construction, safety and security had improved beyond belief in that time. Yet suddenly came a chilling reminder that motor racing indeed remained a hazardous profession.

Even so, Senna's death slammed into the sport's solar plexus in a manner only previously experienced

Poignant moment. Less than a lap before the accident, Senna powers ahead pursued by Michael Schumacher's Benetton, Gerhard Berger's Ferrari, Damon Hill's Williams, the Sauber of Heinz-Harald Frentzen, Nicola Larini's Ferrari, Mika Hakkinen's McLaren and Karl Wendlinger's Sauber. They are passing the scene of the accident which claimed the life of F1 novice Roland Ratzenberger just 24-hours earlier.

when the legendary Jim Clark was killed in a second-division F2 race at Hockenheim in the spring of 1968. Moreover, like Clark's death, there was an undercurrent of trembling uncertainty among Senna's contemporaries. If Ayrton could be killed, nobody was safe.

"I am in a state of total shock," said Nigel Mansell, who was practising at Indianapolis when he heard the news. "Ayrton and I shared some of the most exciting races ever staged, and it is impossible to put into words what a sad loss to motor racing this is."

It was a tragedy that touched motor racing in the way that the death of the "Busby Babes" in the 1958 Munich air disaster ripped the heart out of British soccer. Senna was at the start of his eleventh season of Formula One racing, and over those ten previous

seasons he had triumphed in no fewer than forty-one Grands Prix, a record exceeded only by his colleague and long-time rival Alain Prost, and won three World Championships. At the start of 1994 he left the McLaren team, for which he'd won those titles in 1988, 1990 and 1991, and switched to the rival Williams squad in a quest for his fourth crown. Now the story was over, but the legend was just beginning.

Senna was one of the most motivated, driven and highly focussed men ever to climb into the cockpit of a racing car. He was blindingly fast, totally committed and overwhelmingly competitive. Winning was everything to this deeply religious, introspective and loyal family man. He indelibly stamped his enigmatic, sometimes volatile, personality on an entire decade of dramatic action

Joyless moment. Michael Schumacher (centre) wipes away a tear after winning the 1994 San Marino Grand Prix flanked by Nicola Larini (left), who finished second, and a pensive third placemen, Mika Hakkinen. By then they all knew the seriousness of Senna's crash.

Homecoming. Senna's coffin is carried atop a fire engine from São Paulo International airport to the state legislative assembly where it would lie in state before his funeral on Thursday, 5 May 1994.

in this most spectacular of international sports.

On the Monday after the accident, Roland Ratzenberger's father, Minardi team driver Pierluigi Martini and Brazil's ambassador to Italy, Orlando Carbonar, all paid their last respects to Senna at the Bologna hospital. Once the medical and legal formalities had been completed, Senna's coffin, draped with the green-and-yellow Brazilian flag, left for Bologna airport in a black Mercedes hearse. Hundreds of fans, many in tears, who lined the route. A bouquet of flowers outside the mortuary carried a simple message: "Dear Senna. Always in our hearts."

> *President Itamar Francio declared that there would be three days of national mourning.*

An Italian air-force DC-9 was waiting to fly the coffin to Paris to connect with the scheduled Varig flight that would take it on to São Paulo. The emotion of the occasion was overwhelming.

However, the send-off by the Italian fans was

nothing to the scenes that greeted the arrival of Senna's coffin in his home town. Since before dawn thousands of weeping Brazilians had been waiting at the airport for a glimpse of the casket, which was carried on a scarlet fire engine to the São Paulo state legislative assembly, where it would lie in state for the next 48 hours.

President Itamar Francio declared that there would be three days of national mourning, and the Brazilian flag flew at half-mast on all government buildings across the grieving country. Charles Marzanasco, a spokesman for the Senna family, had appealed on the radio for people to stay away from the airport. "The best way to show your love and respect for Senna is to go in an orderly fashion to the legislature building," he said. His words were ignored: the whole of São Paulo came to a halt as crowds lined the streets.

"I just can't believe he's gone," sobbed one young woman. "I keep hoping I'll wake up and discover it's all been a nightmare." Another teenage girl committed suicide in her acute distress "so that she could be with Senna."

For Europeans, spoiled for choice with a galaxy of stars competing in a wide variety of sports, it was difficult to grasp, let alone comprehend, the intensity of the loss felt by Brazil over the death of the great racing driver.

Since the legendary Juan Manuel Fangio embarked for Europe in the late 1940s, South America has always been a decisive and influential force in Grand Prix racing. Fangio went on to win five World Championships, a record achievement that lasts to this day. In 1993, when Senna won at Interlagos, the veteran Argentinian ace, now frail and in his eighties, appeared on the rostrum to add his own congratulations.

It was an enormously emotional moment for Ayrton. He admired and respected Fangio immensely. In Ayrton's mind he would always be number one. To receive such a personal accolade from the eighty-one-year-old legend was enough to bring tears to his eyes as he took Fangio in his arms and embraced the dignified, white-haired old man. It was a fascinating snapshot of the private Senna, the sensitive and considerate man who so often hid these qualities under an apparent veneer of steel.

In 1970 Brazil became represented on the Championship trail by Emerson Fittipaldi. By 1972, when Senna was tweve years old, he became São Paulo's favourite as the youngest man ever to win the F1 World Championship, at the age of twenty-five. Fittipaldi would be an inspiration to Senna in his youth and later became a trusted friend and mentor when Ayrton was at the absolute zenith of his F1 career.

On Thursday, 5 May 1994, Emerson Fittipaldi was among the great and the good of international motor racing who acted as pallbearers, walking with Senna's coffin in the stifling heat to São Paulo's Morumbi cemetery. He was accompanied by Gerhard Berger, Alain Prost, Jackie Stewart, his nephew Christian Fittipaldi, Senna's Williams team-mate Damon Hill, Thierry Boutsen, Roberto Moreno, Rubens Barrichello, Derek Warwick, Maurizio Sandro Sala, Mauricio Gugelmin and Hans Stuck.

Unfortunately, the Senna family could not bring themselves to accept the presence of Bernie Ecclestone, the vice-president of motor racing's governing body, at the funeral, and he was turned away. Clearly, grief and emotional turmoil had become inextricably intertwined.

Brazilians said that the event's significance had only ever previously been matched by the massive state funerals for former President Getulio Vargas, who committed suicide while in office in 1954, and Tancredo Neves, who died in 1985 only days before he was due to take over the presidential office. As Senna's coffin was lowered into the ground, there was a fly-past by Brazilian air-force planes, two of which inscribed the letter 'S' high in the sky above São Paulo.

Alain Prost, the retired triple champion who had been through more than his fair share of differences with Senna during his professional career, reflected on how he'd noticed that Ayrton had wanted to talk

Three generations of Grand Prix champions, alone with their thoughts, escort Senna's coffin to its resting place in São Paulo's Morumbi cemetery. From left to right, Emerson Fittipaldi, Alain Prost, Christian Fittipaldi (hidden), Jackie Stewart, Johnny Herbert and Senna's old friend Maurizio Sandro Sala. To the right of the coffin, Gerhard Berger and Thierry Boutsen.

Lest we forget. At the start of the 1994 Monaco Grand Prix pole position was left vacant and only the Brazilian flag marked the spot where Ayrton had started from on no fewer than five occasions during his career.

to him on the day before he died. He felt that they had finally put aside all the bitterness that had clouded their relationship ever since their tense driving partnership at McLaren in 1988 and 1989. "I was proud to compete against him," said the Frenchman. "Professionally, he was the only driver I respected. In Senna's honour I will never sit in a Formula One car again."

Gerhard Berger, meanwhile, returned to Austria immediately after the funeral and carefully considered whether or not to retire from Grand Prix racing. "Ayrton was the best friend I ever had in F1," he admitted, "closer to me than anybody else in the business. During my three years driving with him at McLaren, I came to realize that he was the best, one level higher than the rest of us."

The Williams team, which had returned from Imola to find the railings outside its Didcot base transformed by floral tributes to Senna, remained understandably shell-shocked. For Frank Williams, the man who had given Senna his first chance to drive an F1 car back in 1983, it was almost too much to bear. After years of trying he had at last tempted Senna to drive for his team. Now that dazzling dream had been transformed into a har-rowing nightmare.

Williams ran only a single car for Damon Hill at the Monaco Grand Prix a fortnight after the Imola tragedy. It would have been almost unthinkable to have adopted any other strategy. Senna had won a record six times through the tortuous streets of the fairy-tale seaside Mediterranean principality. His final win had been just twelve months earlier,

at the wheel of a McLaren, with Hill's Williams following him home in second place.

The Grand Prix circus was uncannily subdued. Senna's presence seemed to dominate proceedings from beyond the grave, such was the force of his personality. Added poignancy was given to the occasion just before the start of the race when the drivers assembled at the front of the grid for a minute's silence in memory of Senna and Roland Ratzenberger. In their memory, the first row of the grid had been left vacant, with the Brazilian flag painted on pole position, the Austrian flag on sec-ond place.

The competitors then closed their minds to the memories as best they could and got down to work. After matching his best-ever result with a strong second place in the McLaren–Peugeot, Martin Brundle reflected again on the loss of the man who had been his old sparring partner in 1983, back in the days when they were racing Formula Three. "This has been one of my hardest achievements in motorsport," Brundle reflected. "The soul search-ing was very difficult, especially when my five-year-old daughter came and asked whether it was true that Senna was dead. It was tough, but we all had to face the same thing. Did we want to do this anymore? Is it crazy? It was a very emotional and difficult time."

Damon Hill, whose race ended after a first-corner collision with Mika Hakkinen's McLaren, echoed Brundle's sentiments. "The whole thing is awful, a very sorry situation. The sooner we get away from Monaco and back to a semblance of normality, the better it will be." Damon was finding the spectre of Senna's Monaco success, allied to the fact that his father, Graham, had won the race five times, just too oppressive to bear.

Yet for all the sorrow expressed by the leading lights in motor racing, it was the Brazilian man in the street who most identified with Senna. At the time of his funeral a student, Fernando Machado Lemos, summed up the feelings of the entire nation: "He gave us dignity, and to see him race was a relief from all the corruption, misery and poverty that surrounds us." It was a touching legacy that the rest of the world was hard-pressed to understand.

2

THE MAN WHO WOULD BE KING

An intensity of purpose marked Senna even in his youth as an unusually competitive and single-minded driver. His domination of the South American kart-racing scene signalled what was to follow when he later went to Europe and took the minor-league single-seater classes by storm. Truly, this was a world champion in the making.

(Preceding pages) Waiting for the start. A study in concentration as Senna sits strapped in the cockpit of the Formula 3 Ralt in which he contested the 1983 British Championship with such dramatic success.

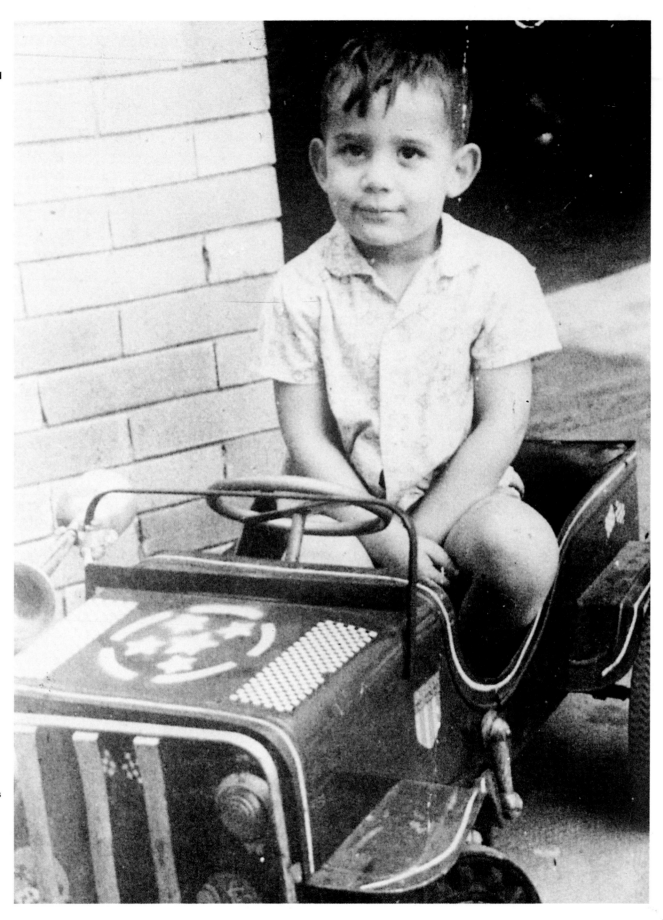

Ayrton as a child. Even at three years of age there is a steely calm about his facial expression. It would become something of a personal trademark in the years ahead.

On 20 March 1960 Neyde, the wife of successful São Paulo businessman Milton da Silva, gave birth to the second of her three children, Ayrton Senna da Silva. They already had one daughter, Viviane, and would later have another son, Leonardo.

When asked in 1993 what he would most like to change about his career in Grand Prix racing, Ayrton replied, "to be able to go back home to Brazil each night during a Grand Prix weekend." It was a telling yardstick by which he judged life's values and an endorsement of the warm, all-embracing family environment in which he had been brought up. By the end of his life Ayrton may have had houses in Monaco and Portugal, but the only true home he had was in Brazil.

Milton da Silva's business interests included a car components and a huge ranch in the Goiania area of central Brazil. When his eldest son was four, da Silva made him his first go-kart, on which he played in the garden of the family's São Paulo home. By the age of

seven the boy was knocking around the farm at the wheel of an old Jeep and soon extended his driving repertoire to tractors and whatever else was available at the time.

In 1973 Emerson Fittipaldi won the first championship Brazilian Grand Prix for Lotus at São Paulo's spectacular Interlagos circuit. That same year, on the kart track within that circuit complex, thirteen-year-old Ayrton da Silva began kart racing on a serious basis.

"He was totally dedicated, obviously a man who was destined for the top. He had great style, great ability."

The split-second, cut-throat world of kart racing has spawned a succession of world champions over the past couple of decades. Fittipaldi himself was a kartist, as was Nelson Piquet, the second Brazilian to win the F1 title crown. In Europe both Alain Prost and Nigel Mansell cut their competition teeth on the spindly little creations that

Senna the kartist. It was in this red-hot crucible of youthful talent that the Brazilian first showed signs of the ability that took him to the pinnacle of his chosen profession.

Leading the pack at Silverstone during his 1981 assault on the British Formula Ford scene. At the wheel of his works-supported Van Diemen RF81, Ayrton won the two most significant national championships, then toyed with retirement when he was told his further advancement depended on finance rather than the obvious merit he believed should be the key.

were propelled by souped-up motorcycle engines.

Senna's portfolio of achievements in this crucible of future Grand Prix talent speaks virtually for itself. In 1977 and 1978 he won the South American Championship and was Brazilian national champion four times in a row from 1978 to 1981. In addition he had his first crack at the karting World Championship at a one-race shoot-out held at Le Mans, France, in 1977. He finished sixth.

Two years later he was back to contest the same event at Estoril, which would be the scene of his first Grand Prix victory only six years later, and came away with second place to the Dutchman Peter Koene. He was second again in 1980 and fourth in 1981, by which time he was seriously involved in single-seater motor racing in Britain.

He was twenty-one years old when he arrived at the Van Diemen factory in rural Norfolk. Founded

by Ralph Firman, a one-time mechanic at the famous Jim Russell Racing Drivers' School based at nearby Snetterton, Van Diemen has a long-established record of building the most competitive cars available for the cut and thrust of Formula Ford 1600, the most successful ever junior category for the aspiring Grand Prix star.

Senna was introduced to Firman by Chico Serra, another Brazilian driver who as a contemporary of Nelson Piquet had been a rising star in the mid-1970s but never quite realized his full potential. For two years Serra had been telling Firman excitedly about another young Brazilian who was currently involved in karting. Now here he was in rural Norfolk about to do the most crucial deal of his fledgling career to date.

"He arrived here with Serra in the middle of January 1981," recalls Firman, "and we all went out

together for dinner. Ayrton didn't speak any English, so all our conversation was routed through Chico. But even at that early stage I could see he had a well-developed business mind. He wanted me to pay him to drive.

"He'd been paid to race karts, so he thought that was the natural thing. I eventually steered him round to a realistic deal, and he began racing with us at the start of that season. He was clearly very good, that was clear from the start. But he was never satisfied – not in the sense of not being gracious but in his continual search for ways to improve. He was totally dedicated, obviously a man who was destined for the top. He had great style, great ability. The rest speaks for itself."

Firman and Senna kept loosely in touch over the years, but inevitably their contact became less frequent as Ayrton's career continued its upward

path. "It's ironic," recalls Firman, "but I hadn't seen him for a couple of years when he suddenly rang me from his car phone for a chat. He'd just arrived back from Japan, and it was just before he went off to Imola."

Others recall Ayrton as being socially a rather shy youngster who kept to himself. "If a group of us went down to the pub, he would come along but stand quietly to one side, sipping his drink and only speaking when he was spoken to," recalls Jim Russell school director John Kirkpatrick.

Ayrton won his third ever car race at Brands Hatch on 15 March 1981, at the wheel of the Van Diemen RF81. By the end of the season he had established himself as the man to beat, winning the two prestigious national British Formula Ford titles. Then, incredibly, he decided that he might retire from racing and go back to Brazil for good. His marriage

Another year, the same story. In 1982 Ayrton took a stranglehold on the Formula Ford 2000 winner's circle. Here he swoops down the hill ahead of the pack at Donington Park on the way to another decisive victory.

On the verge of the Big Time. Senna at the wheel of the West Surrey Racing Ralt RT3, in which he clinched the 1983 British Formula Three championship, the last stopping point before graduation into the Grand Prix set.

to Liliane, his childhood sweetheart, hadn't endured well in the wastes of rural Norfolk. He was irked that further advancement would require him to raise substantial sponsorship. Quite clearly, Ayrton believed he was better than that; he was sure in his belief that progress through the junior ranks should be by talent alone. But that is not the way things work in motor racing.

He returned to São Paulo, and he and Liliane split up soon after. He toyed with the idea of helping his father on the ranch, but after thinking things through and talking with his parents he decided to return to England and fully commit himself to the professional business of motor racing. "I just couldn't resist the attraction of a steering wheel and a racing car," he said many years later. "Up to that point, I had raced largely for fun, and if I had not come back to England, I would probably have continued racing just as a hobby in Brazil."

Shortly before the start of the 1982 season Ayrton

phoned Ralph Firman and did a deal to drive a Van Diemen Formula Ford 2000 car in both the British and European Championships. If he had made his mark on FF1600 the previous year, he now utterly and completely dominated the next rung of the ladder. He won twenty-one of the twenty-seven races contested, including wins in front of the Formula One fraternity in Grand Prix supporting races held at Zolder, Hockenheim and Osterreichring.

At the end of 1982 Ayrton had his first Formula Three drive at Thruxton in a non-championship event. He started from pole position and won easily. He was now poised for the final phase before entering the Grand Prix milieu. Formula Three was the last stepping stone to the Big Time.

With wings and slick tyres, a Formula Three car is effectively a Formula One machine in miniature. It is relatively low powered, so the onus is on the man in the cockpit to drive smoothly, neatly, to extract the maximum amount of grip at all times. In 1983

Ayrton contested the British national F3 championship – with the eyes of the Grand Prix world firmly focussed on his efforts.

Senna drove for the West Surrey team run by the highly respected Dick Bennetts. His Ralt–Toyota RT3 kicked off the season in champion style: the rising Brazilian star won the first nine races on the trot. It was a formidable display of domination, but increasingly he began to experience opposition from a young Englishman at the wheel of an identical machine fielded by the rival Eddie Jordan team.

"I was just a kid from Norfolk," recalls Martin Brundle, now one of Britain's top Grand Prix drivers. "The family garage business in Kings Lynn generated the finance for me to go racing. I'd had my first season of F3 in 1982, and during the following winter everybody kept asking me, 'How are you going to beat Senna?' Frankly, I hardly knew who they were talking about."

As it transpired, the competitive rivalry between the rich man's son from São Paulo and the garage owner's lad from north Norfolk produced such a season of intense competition that it's still talked about enthusiastically more than a decade later. At first it seemed as though Brundle was overawed by Senna. Once he finally beat him in a race, the battle became more evenly balanced and was carried all the way to the final round of the twenty-race series.

When they were squared up for the final confrontation on the Thruxton airfield circuit near Andover, each man

He was given his first test at the wheel of a Grand Prix car by Frank Williams mid-way through his F3 title season.

knew pretty well the qualities of his opponent. Senna had, perhaps grudgingly, come to regard Brundle as a serious rival. Brundle, on the other hand, had perhaps come to understand the level of commitment that would be required to carry the momentum of his own career forward to F1.

(Above) Decisive moment. Powering up to the chicane at Thruxton in the final round of the 1983 British F3 series, Senna is already pulling away from the pack as championship rival Martin Brundle – car no. 1 – battles to pass Davy Jones for second place. (Right) Senna with Brundle on the winner's rostrum at Thruxton after the Brazilian clinched the 1983 British F3 title.

Running ahead of Senna was no guarantee Brundle would stay there. At Oulton Park, Senna "thought he saw a gap," and the two Ralts ended up piled atop the other off the road in a tangle of debris. "The bottom of his car's side-pod ended up resting on my shoulder," said Brundle a decade later. "I led the race, but he thought he could see a gap. Sounds familiar, eh? I didn't think there was one. The marshals actually had to lift his car off mine before I could climb out."

During the week prior to the last race of the season Brundle was working in his father's car-showroom, earning his daily bread. Senna, by contrast, was in Italy, watching a brand new F3 engine being prepared on the test bed – just for the final shoot-out.

Senna won the race and the title. But Brundle recalls just how generously his young Brazilian rival behaved after the race. "After all the nonsense and the rivalry we went through – and, believe me, I sometimes got the impression that Ayrton thought the British motor-racing establishment was ganging up on him – he was truly magnanimous," Brundle remembers. "On the rostrum it was quite emotional.

He told me I was the best British driver since Jim Clark."

Senna was clearly in the fast lane heading towards his first F1 drive. He was given his first test at the wheel of a Grand Prix car by Frank Williams midway through his F3 title season. Then he and Brundle tested a McLaren as their prize for a season of endeavour in that junior category. Eventually Senna signed for Toleman while Brundle joined him in the graduate's class in a berth with Tyrrell. At the start of 1983 several F1 teams had been keen to bankroll Senna's F3 season in return for an option on his services. He refused them all, wanting his independence. "If I win, then I will have the choice," he said perceptively. It was a creed to which he remained loyal throughout his career.

Whenever he was asked whether he was aiming for the all-time record number of victories, he would neatly deflect the inquiry by saying: "If I concentrate hard to win each race, the championships and the records may follow." To him it was an entirely logical process, one flowing naturally as a consequence of the other. His confidence was amazing, both in its intensity and its control.

Ten years further along their career paths Brundle is amused to recall what amounted to a re-run of their Oulton Park collision during the 1993 Italian Grand Prix at Monza. Brundle's Ligier was pushed off the road at the Variante Ascari by Senna's McLaren. It was a big impact, and both drivers ended up in the sand trap, out of the race.

"He came running over to my car at Monza with

Senna's prize for winning the British F3 series was a test in this F1 McLaren–Ford at Silverstone. By this point he had already sampled an F1 Williams at Donington Park and his speed in the McLaren hardly came as a surprise.

(Left) Senna consults with McLaren chief Ron Dennis – behind car – during that crucial test. Just over four years later the two men entered into a World Champion-ship winning partnership that yielded 35 Grand Prix wins and three title crowns. (Below) The eyes of a winner. Senna sits impassively behind the wheel of the F1 Mc-Laren-Ford while it is refuelled during his test session with the car in late 1983. It was the start of something big.

the speed of a man who wanted to thump me," says Brundle with a grin, "but all he wanted to do was to check I wasn't hurt. That was quite touching, I suppose, but once he'd ascertained I was OK, he wasn't in the slightest bit apologetic.

"As we were taken back to the pits in a car, I remarked, 'That's a pity, I really needed that third place.' He just shrugged and said, 'Well, we all needed the points.' Then I said, 'It looks like you've lost the chance of the Championship,' and he replied, 'No, he [Prost] still needs one more point.' And he was absolutely right. He'd had it all worked out in his head."

"To be honest," continues Brundle, "I didn't really know Senna well. In fact, I don't think many people got to. But I have been inspired by his example throughout my career. There's no question about that. Absolutely inspired."

GRAND PRIX APPRENTICESHIP

The critics said he was trying to run before he could walk. But the critics were wrong. Senna's rise through the Grand Prix ranks was relentless. Outgrowing the Toleman team in 1984, he switched to Lotus, where he spent the next four seasons. By the end of 1987 his stature was such that he had also moved beyond Britain's one-time most successful Formula One team.

(Preceding pages)
Heading for his
first World Cham-
pionship point. At
the wheel of the
Toleman–Hart
TG183B on his way
to sixth place in
the 1984 South
African Grand Prix
at Kyalami.

Grand Prix novice.
Senna dressed for
action in his
Toleman F1 team
overalls at the start
of 1984.

ernie Ecclestone is the most powerful man in international motor racing. As the commercial driving force behind the sport's multinational television coverage, which now extends to over one hundred countries, he is a vice-president of the sport's governing body, the F.I.A., as well as president of the Formula One Constructors Association.

For many years he was also owner of the Brabham Formula One team. In 1984 he was keen to have Senna drive for him, but it never came off. Ecclestone's established number-one driver was another Brazilian, Nelson Piquet, who by curious coincidence had snubbed Senna when he was an up-and-coming FF2000 driver and sought to gain an

early stage in his career Senna knew precisely where he wanted to go. And how he intended to get there.

"I will do everything for you," he told Alex Hawkridge, managing director of the Toleman Group car-transportation empire that owned the Grand Prix team. "Every time I get into your car I will give you one-hundred per cent effort. But if I eventually decide the car is not competitive, I will go to another team. And if you try to prevent me from leaving, I will retire from motor racing."

Senna made his F1 debut at the wheel of a Toleman TG183B in the Brazilian Grand Prix at Rio de Janeiro. He qualified an excellent sixteenth but lasted only until the eighth lap of the race when he

First Grand Prix start. Senna's Toleman–Hart (no. 18) piles into the first corner of the 1984 Brazilian Grand Prix pursued by fellow F1 debutant Martin Brundle's Tyrrell (no. 3). Ayrton failed to finish, but his old F3 rival came home fifth on his debut.

introduction to his more celebrated colleague at the 1982 Belgian Grand Prix. "I don't know whether Nelson eventually vetoed it," said Senna much later, perhaps slightly tongue-in-cheek, "but if he did, I can't say I would have blamed him."

In the event Senna joined the Toleman F1 which was later bought by Benetton as the basis of their current highly competitive operation. Even at this

retired with loss of turbocharger-boost pressure. He was not remotely satisfied with his showing.

The second race of the year was the South African Grand Prix at Kyalami. There Senna qualified thirteenth and finished sixth, despite losing the Toleman's nose-cone when he hit some debris on the main straight while scanning his instruments to check out another slight turbo-boost problem. This impromptu change left the car's steering tiresomely heavy, but he struggled on to his first Championship point, exhausting himself so much that he had to be lifted from the car once the battle was over.

Up to now Toleman had been using their 1983 chassis, previously driven by Englishman Derek Warwick, who had now moved on to the French works Renault team. For the upcoming season they were pinning their hopes on the all-new TG184, which was already nearing completion at the team's Oxfordshire factory. But Senna and his team-mate, the former motorcycle ace Johnny Ceccoto, had to make do with their older cars through the Belgian Grand Prix at Zolder, where Ayrton wound up seventh, and the San Marino G.P. at Imola. Senna had never competed at Imola, so was understandably keen to get in as many practice laps as possible.

When he arrived at the circuit, however, he was informed that the Toleman management in England

Supporting cast – for now. Alain Prost (centre) has just won the 1984 Portuguese Grand Prix and Niki Lauda (left) has clinched the Championship. Senna, to the right of FIA President Jean-Marie Balestre, finished third in the Toleman–Hart to lay down a decisive marker for his future achievement.

had ordained that the cars should not compete. A dispute between the team and Pirelli, their tyre suppliers, resulted in the cars failing to contest Friday's first practice session. Ayrton finally got out onto the circuit on Saturday, encountered technical problems and failed to qualify for the only time in his Grand Prix career. In the aftermath of this

commercial row Toleman switched to Michelin rubber in time for the French Grand Prix at Dijon–Prenois, where Senna continued his disappointing run of results with the old car by retiring with engine failure.

Already there were signs that Senna was outgrowing the team. Since Toleman's graduation into F1 at the start of the 1981 season, the team had attracted much praise for initiative and innovation. Lacking support from a major engine manufacturer, it had commissioned the Essex-based engine specialist Brian Hart to build a bespoke 1.5-litre four-cylinder turbocharged engine for its exclusive use.

The next three seasons were a struggle. Turbo technology was expensive and complicated. Hart had precious little to learn in terms of engineering knowledge but applying that know-how to the point where hard results were delivered – especially against major players such as Ferrari, Renault and Honda – took cash. And Toleman was rarely ever overflowing with that particular commodity.

Derek Warwick grew with the team as one of the family. But by the end of 1983 the pleasant Hampshire driver had outgrown what Toleman had to offer; Senna would take about six months to do likewise. From the start of his relationship with Toleman he displayed a finely honed analytical mind. His retention of minute detail was quite remarkable. He could assimilate information, then throw it up in technical debriefs many months later. In the paddock it was almost as if he was stalking his car, creeping up on it when it wasn't expecting him, so that it would reveal all its inner secrets.

Immediately after the French race, Toleman settled down to test the new TG184 in earnest. At Monaco Senna qualified an excellent twelfth, benefiting from a very promising new specification engine that Brian Hart had made available for the first time.

On race day at Monaco in 1984, it rained. And rained. The glizty, sun-soaked town was transformed

(Left) Senna on his Formula One debut with the chunky Toleman–Hart TG183B in the 1984 Brazilian Grand Prix at Rio. (Right) Same driver, same place, different car. Twelve months later Ayrton was strapped into the cockpit of the sleek Lotus–Renault 97T. The winning would begin that year.

into a bleak, uncompromising misery. Low cloud obscured from view the Ranier's Palace atop the headland overlooking the harbour. Nightmarish wasn't the word.

In every world-class sportsman's career there is a key moment, a turning point at which even the sceptics agree they can see the stuff of which legends are made. That Monaco Grand Prix was such a moment for Senna. Up to then he had the obvious credentials, he had the promise. But now, at the wheel of a Grand Prix car, he gave us a taste of what was to come in the ensuing decade.

Alain Prost led from the start, the Frenchman easing his red-and-white McLaren–TAG smoothly into the first corner at the head of the pack. At the end of the opening lap Prost was comfortably ahead, pursued by Nigel Mansell's Lotus–Renault, the Ferraris of Rene Arnoux and Michele Alboreto, Niki Lauda's McLaren, Keke Rosberg's Williams–Honda, Jacques Laffite's Williams – and Senna, having already made up three positions from his starting place.

By the end of lap seven Senna's Toleman was up to seventh place. He was picking off his rivals with all the assurance of a veteran. On lap 11 Mansell managed to squeeze ahead and began to edge away from Prost's McLaren, but next time round Senna was up to fifth. On lap 16 he was third and still going like a rocket, promoted almost immediately to second place when Mansell's Lotus snapped out of his control on the greasy track surface and rattled into the clutches of the unyielding guard rail.

The race had been scheduled to run over a full seventy-seven lap distance, but the rain was coming down in stair rods by the time the lap 30 mark hove into view. Visibility was terrible, yet still Senna closed relentlessly on Prost's McLaren. One didn't have to be a mathematician to see that Prost, grappling with new carbon-fibre brakes that just wouldn't warm up to their proper working temperature in the cool conditions, was a sitting duck.

Only the intervention of the clerk of the course brought the chase to an end. That official was former F1 racer Jacky Ickx, a man who knew more than most about Grand Prix racing in the rain. Twelve years earlier he'd splashed round Monaco in a Ferrari

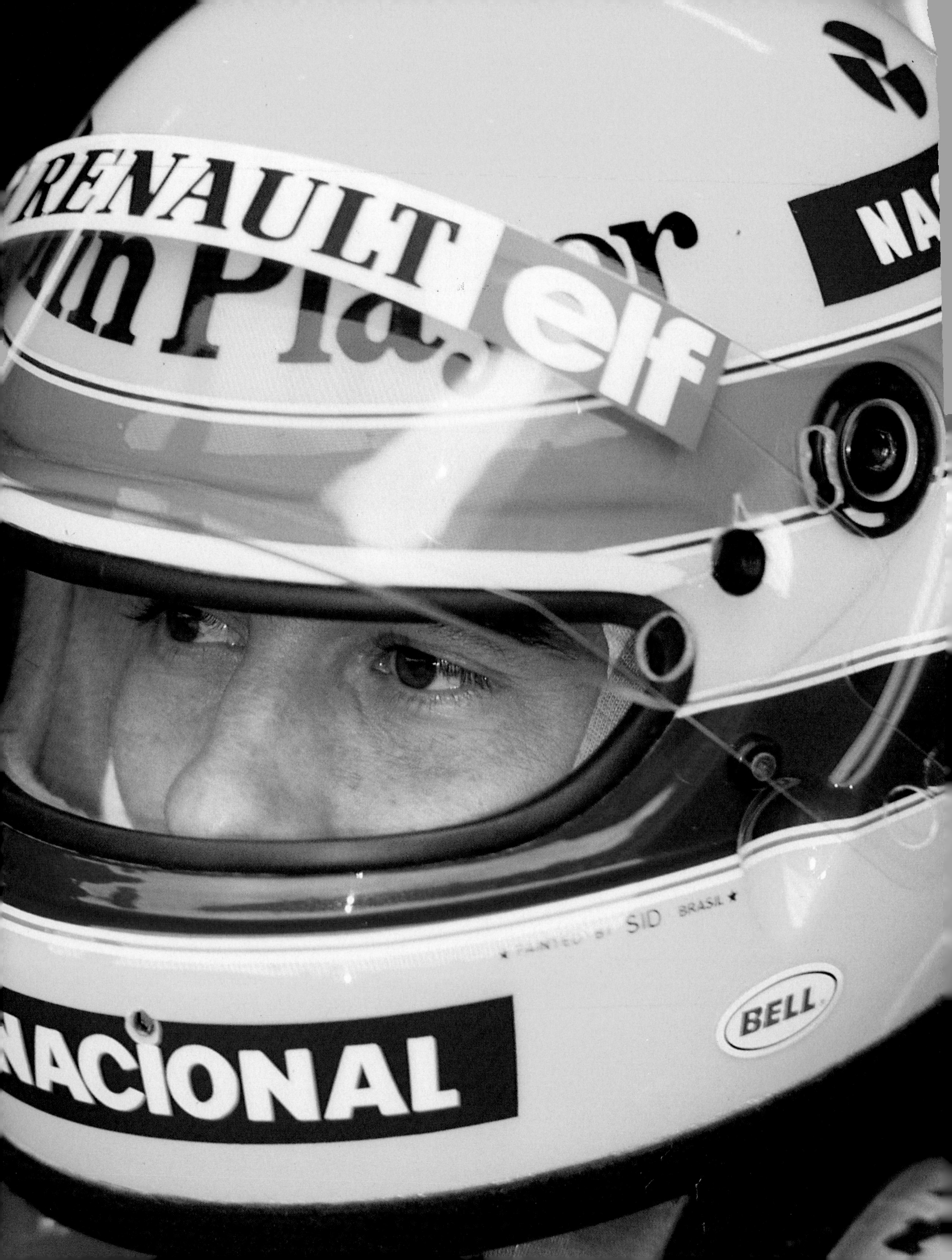
RENAULT
elf
SID
BRASIL
BELL
NACIONAL

to take second place behind outsider Jean-Pierre Beltoise's BRM. Now he decided that the 1984 edition of the classic event had gone on long enough.

At the end of lap 32 Ickx instructed that the red flag be shown at the start-finish line. Prost took the flag with Senna surging past his McLaren only yards after the line. However, as the rules in such circumstances decree that the result is judged by the order on the lap prior to the red flag, Prost won officially by just over seven seconds.

The writing was now on the wall. Senna had stretched the Toleman's performance envelope almost to the breaking point. From then on it was clear that he was destined for better equipment. Sure enough, his relative inexperience would lure him into the odd driving error during the balance of the season, but a storming third place behind Lauda's McLaren and Warwick's Renault in the British Grand Prix at Brands Hatch would serve to confirm what we'd all seen at Monaco.

Senna also increasingly displayed an ice-cold confidence that could chill those around him. On the rostrum at Brands Hatch, Warwick, Lauda turned to the Brazilian to offer the hand of congratulation. Senna's response took him aback. "You were bloody lucky I didn't catch you," said he. And he wasn't joking.

The rival Lotus team was by now sizing up Senna with a view to offering him a contract for 1985. They were planning to drop Nigel Mansell, who hadn't really hit it off with Peter Warr, the team manager, and negotiations began in earnest by the start of August. By the end of that month rumours began to spread that Senna was on the move.

On the morning of the Dutch Grand Prix at Zandvoort, Sunday, 26 August, I went into the Toleman garage and asked Senna directly if it was true he would be joining Lotus for 1985. He looked at me for a moment and said, "Are you mad?"

Inadvertently, I had stumbled on an embarrassing situation. Senna had a nominal three-year contract with Toleman, which though containing the familiar 'buy-out' clause, stipulated that he would have to reach a financial settlement with his current employers before any negotiations with another team could be pursued in detail. According to Toleman,

these terms had been breached. The situation was not helped by a somewhat patronizing statement in the Lotus press release revealing that Senna would be joining their team in 1985 that read: "He [Senna] will, of course, continue to drive for Toleman for the rest of the season." Alex Hawkridge was infuriated by this lofty piece of sledgehammer diplomacy. Peter Warr then backtracked slightly, adding, "I have received the necessary assurances from Ayrton Senna that he will be able to fulfil the obligations and undertakings he has given in the contract he signed with us."

Toleman counterattacked by suspending Senna from the Italian Grand Prix at Monza. This tense caesura, however, would not affect the course of F1 history: Senna was back in the cockpit for the last two races of the season, crashing at the first corner in the Grand Prix of Europe at Nurburgring.

He rounded off his career as a Toleman driver with a brilliant third place to the McLarens of Prost and Lauda in the Portuguese Grand Prix at Estoril. It was a performance that represented the absolute pinnacle of the Toleman–Hart team's achievement; better, some said, even than Monaco.

By that point Brian Hart had been long convinced that Senna's ability easily outstripped the technical potential of the Toleman. "I'd seen the first signs of it at a test session we ran at Donington Park just after the Brazilian Grand Prix," he recalls. "The technical feedback he was offering was astounding from a guy who'd done just a single Grand Prix. Even then I think we knew that the bloke was going all the way to the top. But I think the clincher was the British Grand Prix, where he decisively outdrove several people whom he had no right to be ahead of in the car-engine combination we provided him with."

Having correctly identified that the Lotus–Renault combination would best serve his career ambitions in 1985, Senna duly sealed the deal. But for a man so obviously passionate about his chosen calling, he remained objective enough to agree to joint number-one status with Elio de Angelis, the established senior

He stamped his superiority on the Lotus team with a masterly first Grand Prix victory in the second race of the 1985 season.

The eyes have it. Senna's capacity for concentration became legendary. His dark brown eyes had an intensity that could hypnotize all those around him.

driver who was the team's strength. Even at the time he joined Lotus there was little doubt that Senna was the superior competitor. Yet he lacked experience and shrewdly judged that joint number-one status would enable him to learn the ropes while reducing the pressure. But he decisively stamped his superiority on the team with a masterly first Grand Prix victory in the second race of the 1985 season. The venue was Estoril, the circuit where he had finished third for Toleman at the end of the previous season.

Starting from a comfortable pole position, Senna's Lotus 97T sped serenely to what was rightly hailed as one of the great wet weather victories of the decade. In winning this Portuguese Grand Prix he displayed such obvious assurance in the appalling conditions that his rivals were simply left as floundering, second-rate also-rans.

Even when it came to the task of picking his way through the tail enders, Senna's concentration did not flag for a moment, despite an involuntary trip down the grass on one spectacular occasion. His rational capacity to understand what his car was doing projected an image of false modesty. "They all said I made no mistakes," he said later, "but that's not true. On one occasion I had all four wheels on the grass, totally out of control, but the car just came back on the circuit. "Everybody said 'fantastic car control,'" but that was not the case. It was just pure luck" – not something that Ayrton Senna would have to rely on too frequently during his subsequent career.

It soon became clear that one of the most outstanding facets of Senna's ability as a racing driver was his capacity for instant recall in microscopic detail. He could sit in the cockpit of his car and think his way, inch-by-inch, round a given circuit, working

Proving the pedigree. Senna en route to his maiden victory in the rain-soaked 1985 Portuguese Grand Prix. After this tour-de-force there was no questioning his absolute star quality.

out where he could shave off a few tenths of a second. "He was a man who was frighteningly and single-mindedly devoted to success," recalls Lotus team manager Peter Warr. "In my mind he was the most complete racing driver since Jimmy Clark."

The Lotus–Renault 97T was unquestionably a very good car, but not quite good enough even for Senna to string together a successful onslaught on the World Championship. This was a time at which the competitive performance of the 1.5-litre turbocharged engines was dictated largely by their fuel efficiency. The Renault V6s had the power, but they could not quite match the McLaren–TAGs

or, increasingly, the Williams–Hondas in this one key area.

This was obvious to Senna, and his mood was not improved by accusations that his exuberance with the cockpit turbo-boost control, the operation of which could produce additional spurts of power at tactical moments – albeit at a cost in terms of fuel consumption – caused him to run the Lotus's tank prematurely dry. On two occasions, at Imola and Silverstone, he was contesting the lead with Prost's McLaren when he ran short of juice. But Lotus was quick to defend him on this particular score. Senna had more sense than to voluntarily put him-

Ready to go. With black-and-gold overalls topped off by a distinctive yellow crash helmet, Senna cut a formidable figure during his first years at Lotus. One sight of that helmet in a rear-view mirror was sufficient to unsettle his rivals.

self in a position where he was seen to run out.

This was the year in which he developed a stranglehold on pole position, qualifying fastest at no fewer than seven races during his first season with Lotus. At Monaco this was not without its problems. After Senna secured a crucial first-place starting position, his rivals accused him of deliberately blocking their efforts to unseat him. Naturally, Senna vigorously denied this. However, I witnessed one occasion when, inadvertently or by chance, he held up Niki Lauda's McLaren when the Austrian was on a quick lap. Lauda, one of the most phlegmatic and controlled individuals ever to be strapped into a Grand Prix car, emerged from the cockpit absolutely fit to be tied. I never saw him more furious in his entire career.

Ironically, this was a race at which Senna's acute sense of mechanical perception told him that he was in trouble even before the start. During the half-hour race-morning warm-up session, he admitted that he had missed a gear-change and slightly over-revved the engine. Lesser drivers might have shrugged such an incident aside and then been surprised when the engine failed. Not Senna. He went to the start-line suspecting that the cutting edge of his Renault engine's performance had probably been compromised. He was right: after sixteen laps the engine broke down.

This was the time at which computer telemetry was increasingly being used to monitor engine performance. But having Senna in the cockpit was increasingly like having the services of a human computer. Any driver could read the cockpit instrumentation, but Ayrton could assimilate its implications and alter his driving technique accordingly.

It was becoming clear not only that was he a genius in terms of competitive ability but that he had the remarkable ability to 'think on his feet' at speeds up to 175 mph when it came to interpreting precisely what his car was doing. Lotus engineer Gerard Ducarouge summed it up perfectly when he said: "With Ayrton, we don't need telemetry."

In 1985 Senna still brought to his racing the fresh,

> *We all saw signs of this unfettered exuberance – and his almost shy, formal politeness.*

38

uninhibited joy of youth. It was all new to him and he loved it with unabashed passion. We all saw signs of this unfettered exuberance – and his almost shy, formal politeness.

In the paddock at Rio that year, I was chatting to a handful of my colleagues from the British press. Suddenly Ayrton was at our shoulders. After shaking hands politely he said, "I hope you're having a nice time in my country. If there is anything you need, or anything I can help with, please ask me." It was delivered with the genuine civility of a man who'd been brought up to keep quiet rather than mouth platitudes he didn't mean.

Later that summer a turbo pipe came loose in the Canadian Grand Prix at Montreal, forcing Senna to play catch-up. For most of the race he ran in nose-to-tail formation with Keke Rosberg's Williams–Honda, which had also been delayed. To hear him enthuse about Rosberg's driving style again reflected a delightful lack of pretence.

Senna won only one other race in 1985, the Belgian Grand Prix at Spa Francorchamps. But by the end of that season it was clear that he was stretching Lotus to its maximum, demanding more and more from a team that was hard-pressed to keep pace with his uncompromising standards.

Lotus had been one of the greatest names in post-war British Formula One racing history. Throughout the 1960s and 1970s, under the dynamic leadership of its founder, Colin Chapman, they were consistent front-line operators, winning no fewer than seven World Championships. But Lotus dropped from the competitive high wire in the late 1970s, and the apparent decline was accelerated by Chapman's death in December 1982.

Seen from a purely historical perspective, Senna's three-year spell with Lotus didn't stop the rot, but it certainly put a brake on the team's decay. The team would be there or thereabouts right through to the end of 1987, when Ayrton finally took his leave and switched to McLaren.

Lotus has never looked like winning a Grand Prix since. Towards the end of 1985 one man was afforded a unique, fleeting insight into what made Senna such a special performer at the wheel. John Watson, a veteran of a decade's Grand Prix en-

deavour, was having his last ever F1 drive deputized in the McLaren team for Niki Lauda, who had injured his wrist. The occasion was the Grand Prix of Europe at Brands Hatch, and Watson was just slowing his McLaren after a qualifying run on the first day of the meeting.

"I came through Westfield Bend into Dingle Dell," he recalls very precisely, "when I saw a black car coming up in my mirrors and moved off-line to let it past. It was Senna, and I then witnessed something that few people could ever have been privileged to see from such close quarters.

"As he came past me, not only was his car carrying so much speed, but he seemed to be braking, blipping the throttle, changing gear and throwing his car into Westfield Bend all at the same time. And at absolutely awesome speed.

"The Lotus was dancing absolutely on tippy toes, on the very limit of adhesion, but he displayed this remarkable ability to retain his composure in such extreme situations. I reckon I saw something very special that day: it was a little glimpse of his genius."

Senna's relentless commitment to success continued into 1986, when he resolutely refused to have British driver Derek Warwick alongside him as the second driver. It wasn't that he feared Warwick; he had no doubt that he could handle the Englishman, but he still believed Lotus was not up to the job of preparing two front-line cars. Painful though it might be to concede the point, Senna was probably right.

Rare error. Even the greatest occasionally make a mistake, as this shot of Senna's Lotus–Renault 98T spinning wildly over a kerb during practice for the 1986 Hungarian Grand Prix dramatically testifies.

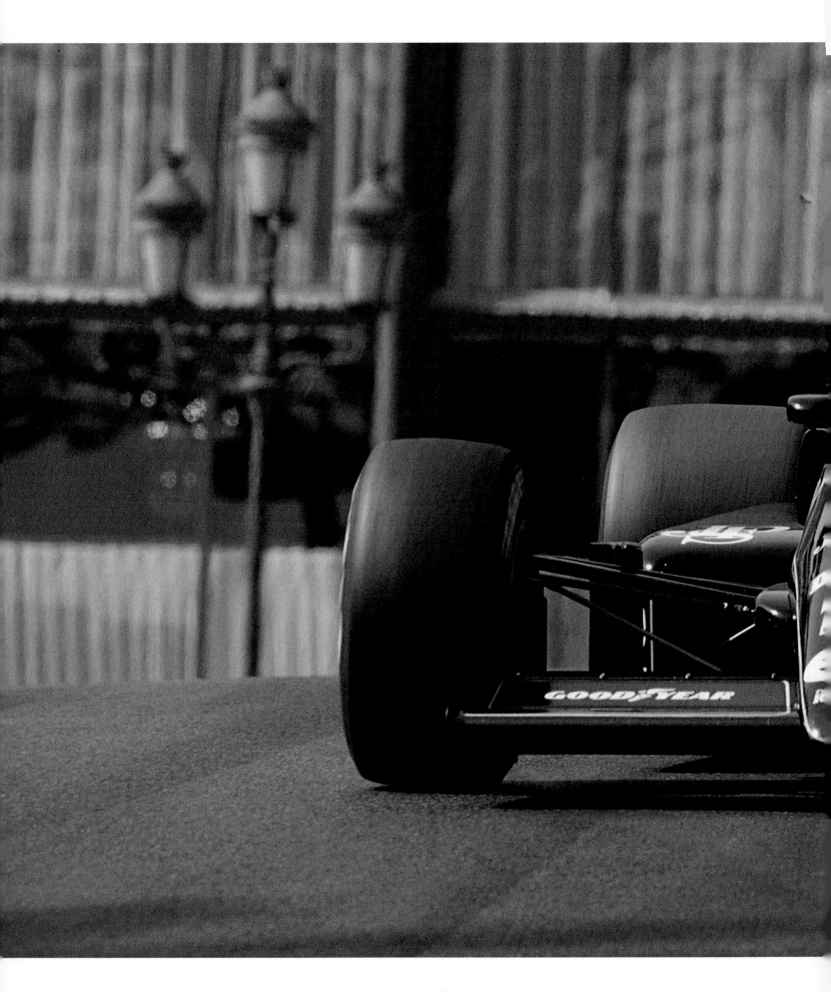

He got his way. The team deferred to his wishes and hired F3 graduate Johnny Dumfries, who is today the multimillionaire Marquis of Bute. Dumfries proved a steady, reliable second-string operator, leaving Ayrton to keep focussed on winning his first World Championship, an ambition that again slipped through his fingers, very largely due to the Renault V6 engine's marginal fuel efficiency compared with its rivals. Yet again.

This, like the Toleman dispute, put Senna on the receiving end of much criticism from the British specialist motor-racing press. These skirmishes, obliquely, offered an added insight into Senna's psyche. If you were his friend and supporter, it seemed, you had to offer unstinting support. Any criticism, however mild and balanced it might appear, meant that you were in the opposition camp. Seeing other people's points of view was never really Senna's strong card. Yet such apparent intolerance was perhaps merely reflective of a self-belief that was so overwhelming that he just couldn't grasp that other people might have views at variance with his own. For a man who was so obviously intelligent this was a curious blind spot.

In 1986 Senna won the Spanish and Detroit Grands Prix. The former was the first such event to be held at the twisting new track at Jerez de la Frontera and has gone down in historical terms as a race that was almost won by Nigel Mansell's Williams–Honda. After a late race stop for fresh

tyres, the gallant Englishman sliced into Senna's remaining advantage to pass the chequered flag virtually level with the Brazilian's Lotus.

After the race Mansell remarked that it was ironic that the start-finish line had been repositioned closer to the final corner. Had it been at its original site, a few metres farther down the circuit, he would have won. The Senna fans, however, preferred to view the outcome from the opposite end of this particular telescope. Their reading of the situation was that Ayrton had everything perfectly weighed up and was letting out the rope as much as he dared, to conserve both his fuel and tyres in the closing moments of the race. It was the closest recorded Grand Prix finish, with Senna ahead by one-hundredth of a second. In his view that was all you needed to know.

His second win of the season came on the equally tricky Detroit street circuit, where despite an early pit stop to change a punctured tyre he judged things perfectly to pull off a memorable victory. It was his first of three wins in Motown, the heart of America's car-building industry.

The latest Lotus–Renault 98T was a superbly competitive tool, and the team began the season determined to give Senna every opportunity of winning his first World Championship. He would be on pole position no fewer than eight times, but with the fuel allowance for each race now slashed from 220 to 195 litres, the need to balance economy of consumption with performance fell into even sharper perspective.

The situation became clearer at Rio after the opening race of the season on Senna's home turf. His Lotus 98T finished second, its tanks almost dry. By contrast, his compatriot Nelson Piquet's Williams–Honda FW11 won convincingly. With fuel to spare.

Renault, whose own works team had been withdrawn from Formula One at the end of 1985, spared nothing in their new role as engine supplier to help Lotus win the Championship. But as Senna's chances slipped away, one could sense that he was becoming more frustrated with the Anglo–French partnership as a whole.

The turbos were flown immediately down to Estoril, fitted to Senna's car, and he duly took pole position for the Portuguese Grand Prix.

After Nigel Mansell's Williams retired, Senna's Lotus 99T assumed the lead at the 1987 Monaco Grand Prix and went on to win. Here he accelerates out of the tight Loews Hotel hairpin on the way to the first of his six wins through the streets of the glamorous Mediterranean city.

43

Bernard Dudot, Renault's highly respected chief engineer, did not work again with Senna until the start of 1994, when he rejoined the Williams team for a few final months before the Imola tragedy. But the Frenchman knew just what was waiting for him in terms of ruthless commitment. Just before the start of the season he recalled his experiences with Senna at the 1986 Portuguese Grand Prix, the race at which Senna's title chances were finally sluiced away when he ran out of fuel on the final lap while running second to Nigel Mansell's winning Williams.

Philippe Coblence, one of Dudot's colleagues, tried some experiments with special new Garrett turbochargers on the test bed in the late summer of 1986. Never one to pass up the opportunity of gaining even the slightest performance edge, Ayrton was immediately anxious to assess their performance once installed in the car.

Senna's second Lotus–Honda win of 1987 came in the Detroit Grand Prix, where the car's computer-controlled active suspension system reduced the physical battering he would have otherwise received on this bumpy, makeshift street circuit.

(Opposite) Dogged concentration. Pulling on his gloves as he prepares to wrestle with the unloved Lotus–Honda 99T in practice for the 1987 Detroit Grand Prix, a race he later won.

The performance of a turbocharged engine is ultimately dictated by the amount of boost pressure an engine will sustain before flying to bits in a hail of white-hot shrapnel. That's putting it a bit basically, perhaps, but suffice to say that Dudot just couldn't believe his eyes when he saw how much boost pressure the engine would sustain equipped with the new turbos. The turbos were then flown immediately

down to Estoril, fitted to Senna's car, and he duly took pole position for the Portuguese Grand Prix almost a second ahead of Mansell. If Dudot and his colleagues expected effusive thanks from the Brazilian, however, they were to be disappointed.

"All Ayrton said was that if he'd known before what we'd put on the engine, he would have driven his qualifying lap differently," he says, laughing. Senna did not mean to be ungracious. He was just so completely immersed in his own job that he naturally assumed that everybody else involved in the programme would offer corresponding levels of commitment as a matter of course.

In 1987 Lotus had the final throw of the dice with Senna. It was now clear that Honda engines were needed, so the team joined Williams in using the powerful Japanese-built V6 turbos. The deal was expedited by Lotus, who agreed to sign Japan's Satoru Nakajima as the number-two driver alongside Senna. Ayrton was now hopeful he could give Mansell and Piquet a genuine run for their money.

Sadly, Senna was to be disappointed. The Lotus 99T was aerodynamically inferior to the rival Williams FW11B, and Ayrton found himself, if anything, at more of a relative disadvantage than he'd been in the final season using Renault engines.

The Lotus 99T was also fitted with computer-controlled 'active suspension', which in simple terms was a system that operated in the way the human brain sends messages to the muscular system. Legs are not springs, so when the brain senses a change in the surface on which it is being asked to walk, it makes instantaneous adjustments and minuscule compensations.

Lotus effectively applied this sensitivity and response to their F1 car's suspension system, to the benefit of ride quality, reduced tyre wear and minimized driver fatigue. Unfortunately, aside from the car's aerodynamic shortcomings, the 'active' Lotus 99T was also too heavy and ponderous. Senna managed to win at Monaco and Detroit, but elsewhere the Lotus–Honda looked a less than ideal tool for the job.

In the British Grand Prix at Silverstone, a race highlighted by Mansell's heroic pursuit of Piquet that saw the Englishman's Williams–Honda surge through

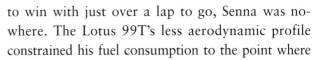

Senna sits patiently in the cockpit of the Lotus–Honda 99T as mechanics work to rectify a minor problem. The car was consistently outclassed by the Williams–Hondas, but Senna always gave one-hundred per cent effort every time he climbed behind the wheel.

In 1987 Lotus had the final throw of the dice with Senna.

to win with just over a lap to go, Senna was nowhere. The Lotus 99T's less aerodynamic profile constrained his fuel consumption to the point where he could only finish third, one lap behind. In terms of comparative ability between Piquet, Mansell and Senna, this was absolute nonsense and a savage indictment of the Lotus–Honda's negative qualities.

To all intents and purposes this was the end of the road for the partnership between Lotus and Senna. It confirmed what Senna already knew, and within a month he had formalized a deal to join McLaren for 1988. Moreover, McLaren would be taking over Williams's supply of Honda engines. The great days of Ayrton Senna's Grand Prix ascendancy were about to begin.

Despite these two victories Senna knew that by his high standards there wasn't much right about the Lotus–Honda 99T. As he discusses the car's performance with his engineers, his expression betrays the frustration of a thwarted World Champion.

Although only 27 years old during the 1987 season, Senna reflected the dynamic motivation and inner drive of a man who knows the best is yet to come – and he has so much more potential to unlock.

CHAMPIONSHIP
GLORY

*During his halcyon years
with McLaren, races and
rivals seemed to surrender to
Senna's intoxicating blend of
raw speed, technical knowledge and total commitment.
He won his first World
Championship in 1988,
followed by two more in
1990 and 1991. After six
years with the team and
restless for a renewed
challenge, however, he quit
McLaren to join Williams.*

49

(Preceding pages)
Straining every
sinew, Senna
presses on in the
lead of the 1988
Italian Grand Prix
at Monza with the
McLaren–Honda
MP4/4. This was a
day on which his
relentless competi-
tiveness caused
him to come un-
stuck, and he
collided with Jean-
Louis Schlesser's
Williams while
lapping the slower
car.

With the McLaren–
Honda MP4/4
prior to the 1988
U.S. Grand Prix at
Detroit, a race he
won even more
decisively than he
had managed for
Lotus the previous
two years.

In the summer of 1987 Ayrton Senna finally sealed a three-year deal to drive for the McLaren team from the start of the following season. In so doing he left a lot of friends at Team Lotus. It was an emotional wrench for the Brazilian driver, as indeed it would be six seasons later when he turned his back on McLaren and switched to Williams.

By then, of course, he would have boosted his total of Grand Prix wins from six to forty-one and added three World Championships to his ever-

handle competing alongside Alain Prost, by then in his fourth season with the team and already the winner of two title crowns.

Drawing on his experience of running beside Niki Lauda in the McLaren squad, John Watson offered Senna his opinion that the best way to deal with Prost would be by stealth rather than by engineering a head-to-head confrontation. Senna listened politely, then surprised Watson by telling him he had other ideas.

A rare relaxed moment between Prost and Senna in an otherwise tense and turbulent partnership for McLaren.

lengthening record of achievements. Former McLaren team driver John Watson, who had witnessed Senna's superlative driving at close quarters round Brands Hatch a couple of years earlier, found himself chatting to Senna about his prospects with McLaren during the summer of 1987. The conversation worked round to how Ayrton would

"He told me he would beat Prost by being fitter, more motivated and more dedicated," Watson recalls. "He said he would make sure he was in a position to drive faster, more consistently, and for longer than Prost could. He meant to beat him convincingly from the front, and I recall thinking, Well, that seems a little optimistic."

McLaren would be moving into a fresh era at the start of 1988. Team chief Ron Dennis had concluded an engine-supply deal with the Japanese Honda company, much to the displeasure of the rival Williams organization, which was having its own supply of Honda engines terminated with one year of their mutual contract still to run.

After witnessing the Williams debacle at Adelaide in 1986, when Nigel Mansell and Nelson Piquet fumbled a vital catch and allowed the Drivers' Championship to fall into Prost's lap like an over-ripe plum, Honda began to question its feelings about the Williams management structure.

Frank Williams had been seriously injured in a road accident early that same season while en route to Nice airport. He was left paralyzed, confined to a

wheelchair, and many months passed before he could even begin to resume any sort of management role in the company that bore his name. Honda got jittery, unable to grasp that the company had a perfectly competent management to continue operating its racing cars, and decided to look elsewhere.

The technical regulations for 1988 reflected the fact that this was a transitional year, closing the era of the complex turbocharged engine prior to the introduction of 3.5-litre non-turbo rules. But for this single season either type of engine was permissible. The rule makers thought that the turbos would be handicapped out of existence when they slashed their fuel capacity from 195 to 150 litres, their boost pressure from 4-bar to 2.5-bar.

McLaren and Honda had other ideas, however,

Ready to go. Strapped tight in the cockpit of the McLaren MP4/4 prior to the start of the 1988 Italian Grand Prix at Monza, a race in which Senna's impulsive streak got the better of him and cost him victory in a collision with a slower car.

and together with Senna and Prost would go on to win fifteen out of the season's sixteen races, a tour-de-force without equal in the sport's history. Prost won three out of the first four races, after which Senna really began to get his championship assault underway. In the two North American races at Montreal and Detroit, Senna was absolutely in a class of his own when it came to ducking and diving through traffic. This was crucial in qualifying when it is necessary to drive absolutely on the limit to achieve a handful of very quick laps. Prost, with two World Championships and many Grand Prix wins under his belt, could not quite motivate himself to take those spectacular risks, even though there could be no questioning his ability as a racer once the green lights came on at the start.

Throughout the summer of 1988, the complexities of the relationship between Prost and Senna began to preoccupy the headlines far more than the technical domination of the McLaren–Honda alliance. If that seemed unfair, it merely mirrored an inevitable trend. With the media interest in Formula One running at fever pitch it was personalities rather than machines that grabbed the headlines.

McLaren actually made quite a fuss of Senna, going out of its way to nanny their new boy in his new and unfamiliar environment. That in itself provided another key to Senna's character: although his outwardly cool countenance would earn him the 'Ice Man' soubriquet, in reality Senna's genius was akin to a volcano on the verge of erupting. Once the lava flow was unleashed, there

Ayrton's first World Championship was firmly in the bag by the 1988 season's finale in Adelaide. Having damaged a wrist playing volleyball on a sun-soaked beach in the fortnight's break following his title clincher at Suzuka, to the detriment of his gear-changing ability, he was content on this occasion to follow Prost home in second place.

(Preceding pages) The dream team prepares for battle. In 1988 Senna – no. 12 – lined up alongside Prost – no. 11 – in the all-conquering Honda–Marlboro–McLaren squad. Here their McLaren MP4/4s prepared for the Spanish Grand Prix at Jerez de la Frontera where Alain won and Ayrton could only manage a troubled fourth.

Glorious moment. Ayrton celebrates clinching his first World Champion-ship title after winning the 1988 Japanese Grand Prix at Suzuka.

was every possibility it might spill out of control.

To get the best out of this overwhelmingly gifted young man McLaren had to keep him simmering just below boiling point. Moreover, because he was so obsessively wrapped up in his chosen profession, insulating him from the stifling media and commercial pressures away from the cockpit soon became every bit as important as furnishing him with the best machinery to get the job done.

Forming an accurate perspective on his relationship with Prost has become a fascinating exercise in retrospective analysis. Even by the middle of 1988 it was not difficult to detect trouble coming, although circumstances obliged Prost to take a strategically deferential role towards the end of the summer.

After returning to Europe determined to mount a dramatic counterattack, Prost won the French Grand Prix before being forced to take a back seat to Senna, who went on to win the British, German, Hungarian and Belgian races in quick succession. It seemed as though the Championship was over. After the Belgian race Alain conceded that it would be virtually impossible to catch Senna in the title chase.

At Monza, however, Senna made a crucial mistake when he tripped over a backmarker, handing the Italian Grand Prix win to Gerhard Berger's Ferrari. Then the pendulum gradually began to swing back in Prost's favour, and the two team-mates arrived at Suzuka for the Japanese Grand Prix each still with a shot at the Championship.

Senna qualified commandingly on pole position, then stalled his engine on the grid. But luck was on his side. The downhill gradient allowed him to bump-start his Honda engine into life and enact a mind-numbing comeback from eighth place on the opening lap to win the race and clinch his first World

Championship. In doing so Senna broke Jim Clark's record of seven wins in a single season, a feat that had stood for twenty-five years.

Those last closing races of the year raised the temperature of the relationship between Prost and Senna. At the start of the Portuguese G.P. at Estoril Senna thought that Alain edged him over to the outside of the circuit in an un-

Only on the day before Senna died did Prost sense a real possibility of an enduring rapprochement with the erstwhile rival.

necessarily brusque fashion as they went into the first corner.

The event was subsequently stopped and restarted

due to a multiple collision further back in the pack. This time Senna made the best start, chopping across his rival going into the first turn. At the end of the opening lap, as Prost swooped alongside him to challenge for the lead, Senna squeezed him so tightly against the pit wall that rival teams quickly withdrew their signalling boards for fear they would strike the Frenchman's McLaren as it shaved by at almost 180 mph.

After the race Prost told Senna that he hadn't

Senna's capacity to absorb information was one of his greatest assets. His concentration is written all over his face as he monitors the performance of his competitors on a portable timing screen while qualifying for the 1989 Mexican Grand Prix.

realized that Ayrton was prepared to risk a fatal accident, and if he really wanted the World Championship that much he could have it. The cracks in the relationship were subsequently papered over behind closed doors, but cracks they remained. Concealed, not repaired.

In 1989, armed with the new Honda 3.5-litre V10 cylinder engine, McLaren would again be a highly competitive force, but the relationship between Senna and Prost deteriorated dramatically. This feud sparked a bitter personal antipathy between the two men that would last until the close of Prost's active racing career at the end of 1993. Only on the day before Ayrton died did Alain sense a real

should have an informal 'no-passing' rule at the first corner. Prost agreed that it would be a great idea. No problems arose at the start when Senna made the best getaway, but the race was soon red-flagged to a halt after a fiery crash involving Gerhard Berger's Ferrari.

At the restart Prost got the jump on Senna, but the Brazilian apparently reneged on the no-passing deal, surging by into the first corner. Alain was infuriated; Ayrton merely shrugged it aside, explaining that he in fact overtook Prost on the straight before the corner rather than at the braking area for the corner itself.

This might have seemed like a fine distinction, but clearly Senna was now giving Prost the tools to

possibility of an enduring rapprochement with the erstwhile rival.

The trouble began at the 1989 San Marino Grand Prix at Imola, where Senna and Prost qualified their McLaren–Honda MP4/5s in first and second places, comfortably ahead of the field. At the first race of the year in Brazil, Senna had been involved in a silly first-corner skirmish with another car, losing his McLaren's nose-cone.

Now Senna proposed that the two team-mates

psychologically bury himself. You could see Alain's point of view. He'd been the rock on which McLaren had operated so successfully ever since the start of 1984. Now he could detect the balance of power shifting decisively in Ayrton's favour. It was, in part, an almost unconscious process. Certainly McLaren team stalwarts, those who worked on the inside preparing the cars, could see the merits and shortcomings of both drivers. Team chief Ron Dennis worked all hours to make the 'dream-team'

partnership work, but after the first few races of 1989 it was clear that the deal was becoming unstitched.

Honda's position as engine supplier has been difficult to judge accurately, but it was certainly a key factor in the equation. Insiders believe that the Japanese engine supplier displayed an inequitable partiality towards Senna. This was perhaps understandable, for he was always perceived as more an 'engine man,' keen on maximizing his performance potential in that area. Prost, by contrast, was a 'chassis man,' one aspect of his brilliance being the ability to adjust the car's handling to an absolute optimum pitch.

Senna, we now know, often relied on copying Prost's chassis set-up – then going faster by using it. Add that to the feeling that he had been betrayed by Senna at Imola, and one can easily understand why Prost announced at the French Grand Prix that he would not be continuing with McLaren in 1990. A couple of months later he announced a deal to join Nigel Mansell at Ferrari.

After Prost won the Italian Grand Prix at Monza, round twelve of the sixteen-race title battle, Senna had slipped twenty points adrift due to a handful of disappointing retirements in the middle of the season. Prost now firmly hinted Honda was favouring Senna with better engines. The Japanese company was aghast at this allegation and, together with McLaren and Prost, issued an absurdly self-conscious joint statement at the Portuguese G.P. indicating that Prost 'deeply regrets the adverse publicity and the resulting embarrassment that have been caused by these actions.' Nobody was taken in, but Senna now went on the defensive behind closed doors. In the author's hearing he urged Honda to persuade Ron Dennis that Prost should be dropped from the McLaren line-up even before the end of the season. "We will be haemorrhaging technical information that he can take with him to Ferrari," said Ayrton angrily.

Needless to say, this was not a realistic option, and the moment passed. The time bomb continued to tick away in terms of the relationship between the two drivers. Finally, at the Japanese Grand Prix, it exploded into shreds, publicly and uncomfortably.

Senna qualified on pole position, but made a last-

The strain and pressure of a committed professional shows on Senna's face as he walks back to the pits after being eliminated from the 1989 Portuguese Grand Prix in a spectacular collision with Nigel Mansell's Ferrari. It served as a graphic reminder to the Brazilian of just what a narrow margin existed between success and tragedy.

minute adjustment to his McLaren's aerodynamic set-up. It proved the wrong way to go and Prost got the jump on him from second place on the starting grid. From then on the two McLarens circulated in nose-to-tail formation, the crowd on tenterhooks as it waited to see how the confrontation would work out.

Senna tried to work it out. In order to wrest the Championship from Prost's clutches he had to win not only here at Suzuka but also at the Australian Grand Prix at Adelaide a fortnight later. But the laps were rolling by and time was running out. Ayrton knew that his only chance to pass would be under-braking for the very tight chicane just before the pits.

On lap 47, with only six to go, Senna made his move. Coming into the braking area at a seemingly impossible speed, Ayrton put his right-hand wheels across the entrance to the pit lane, then ran along the grass and the inside kerb as he forced his way alongside Alain, the two McLarens snaking and weaving with the sheer ferocity of their braking effort. Many times before Prost had given way to avoid a collision in close battles with Senna. The Brazilian was clearly again relying on such a compliant response. But Alain had come to the end of his patience and turned into the corner, unwilling to concede an inch.

The two cars collided and slithered to a halt, absurdly locked together in the middle of the track.

Without a moment's hesitation Alain unclipped his belts and climbed from the car. Ayrton immediately focussed his mind on how to get going again.

Marshals responded to Senna's signals to pull his car back, duly push-started it into action, and the Brazilian was able to resume the chase. Unfortunately, instead of steering through the chicane, Ayrton chose to accelerate through the escape road and out the other side in order to regain the circuit. Despite a quick pit stop to replace a damaged nose section, he went like the wind to pass Alessandro Nannini's Benetton, re-take the lead and win the race.

He was then excluded from the results for missing the chicane, thus handing Nannini the win. Senna simply couldn't believe it. The McLaren team vowed it would fight to the ends of the earth to have Ayrton's victory reinstated.

It wouldn't happen. Prost was World Champion, and Senna found himself with a burning sense of injustice. Those flames of personal indignation would continue to be fanned in his heart. That was the only place I could overtake," he explained, "and somebody who should not have been there just closed the door and that was that. The results as they stand provisionally do not reflect the truth of the race in either the sporting sense or the sense of the regulations. I see this result as temporary.

"Now the matter is out of my hands," Senna went on. "What I have done is done and is correct. From now on, this matter will be in the hands of the lawyers, people who understand the theoretical side. As for the practical side, it was obvious I won on the track." It was a telling barometer of the situation that he refused to mention Prost by name.

Alain was more philosophical. "I must admit that Ayrton is an extremely good driver," he said with masterly understatement. "He is extremely motivated, but in my view he is driving too hard. To be honest, from a personal point of view, it has become absolutely impossible to work with him."

As they sat in the stewards' office at Suzuka after the official adjudication, Prost walked forward and proffered his hand, saying that he was sorry that

McLaren mechanics rush to change tyres on Senna's McLaren MP4/5B during the 1990 Mexican Grand Prix. But there was damage to the rear suspension after a tyre had deflated; retirement was the disappointing outcome.

(Below) Streaking through the infield at Hockenheim, Ayrton's McLaren MP4/5B heads to yet another commanding victory in the 1990 German Grand Prix. (Bottom) Preparing for the 1990 Belgian Grand Prix at Spa Francorchamps where he would win the third of four straight victories on this circuit set amid the pine forests of the Haut Fagnes region.

things had ended this way. Ayrton brushed aside the gesture and told the Frenchman he never wanted to see him again.

The following year life on the Grand Prix trail settled down into its usual routine. Prost got into the swing of things at Ferrari, while Senna got down to work with a new team-mate, Austrian driver Gerhard Berger. A happy-go-lucky Golden Labrador of a man, Berger became one of the few fellow drivers who grew close to Senna. It would be too easy to say Senna liked him only because he knew he could beat him, there was more to it than that. Gerhard's genuinely affable personality struck a chord with the ascetic Brazilian. Senna lightened up

in his company and developed a sense of humour that he had perhaps previously concealed from the view of most people in the paddock.

Senna had won twenty Grands Prix by the end of 1989 and continued to surge through the next season as the man to beat. But Prost's presence at Ferrari raised the competitive stakes as he began to get on a winning roll. By the season's halfway mark he had won four of the eight races to Senna's three and led the title chase by two points. Then Ayrton gradually extended his advantage to the Italian Grand Prix, moving eighteen points clear of his old rival with four rounds of the title chase still to go.

It was at the Monza post-race press conference where the first signs of a rapprochement could be seen. In response to a question inquiring whether or not they were ever going to make their peace, the two men slapped each other playfully on the back. But if Prost thought it was the first step on the road to an armistice, he was to be proved about as wrong as could be.

When the Grand Prix circus pitched tent at Suzuka for the 1990 Japanese Grand Prix, Senna could see his second World Championship title under assault from Prost's Ferrari. In his own mind he had already been robbed of the 1989 title in circumstances that he believed demonstrated the partiality of the sport's governing body. Now, having qualified fastest ahead of Prost in Japan, he was told that pole position for the race would be on the left-hand side of the circuit. To Ayrton this was another example of officialdom favouring the Frenchman.

Prost, though second on the grid, was being handed the incalculable advantage of starting on the racing line, the clean polished section of tarmac on the left-hand side of the circuit. By contrast, Senna would have to start from the dusty, unswept right-hand side of the track, where there would be appreciably less grip for his tyres. On race morning Senna was agitated, preoccupied by this state of affairs. "If Prost gets the best start, then I'm warning him, he'd better not turn in on me, because he isn't going to make it," he was heard to remark to nobody in particular.

Sure enough, Prost got the best start, but Senna

wasn't to be denied. As the Ferrari swung into the first right-hander, Ayrton's McLaren kept coming. In a shower of sparks it rammed the rear of the Italian car, and they both pirouetted off into the sand trap on the outside of the turn. Prost's title hopes were spent, and Senna was champion.

The motor-racing world was stunned. Bitterness and controversy erupted. "It is a scandal that a World Championship should be decided on such a collision," said Jean-Marie Balestre, "and I leave everyone to be their own judge of who is to blame. I am sure all motor-racing fans throughout the

standably furious, convinced that Senna had ruthlessly and deliberately taken him out of the race in order to clinch the Championship. "If everybody wants to drive in this way then this sport is finished," declared Prost. "Senna is completely the opposite in character to what he wants people to believe. He is the opposite of honest. Motor racing is sport, not war.

> *The most frightening thing about the whole episode was that Senna had been prepared to risk his life.*

Split-second from disaster. The start of the 1990 Japanese Grand Prix, with Prost's Ferrari (no. 1) taking its legitimate line into the first corner, with Senna, thwarted in an argument over where pole position should be, coming through regardless to push the Frenchman off the circuit and exact his revenge for an episode 12 months earlier, when the two men, then McLaren team-mates, also collided.

world will feel as frustrated as I do after such an appalling end to the World Championship."

Thankfully, neither driver was hurt, but both cars were badly damaged in the enormous impact, which tore the rear wing off the Ferrari and the left front wheel from the McLaren. Prost was under-

"Technically, I believe we at Ferrari won the World Championship. Losing this way is disgusting. We were not even side by side. If you accept Senna's behaviour then perhaps we will get to a situation in which people will start entering a team with one car specifically intended to push off the opposition to

Another ambition
achieved. Ayrton
on the victory
rostrum after
winning the
Brazilian Grand
Prix at São Paulo's
Interlagos circuit
for the first time,
in 1992.

enable the other guy to win. This man has no value."

Senna responded robustly. "I don't give a damn what Alain Prost says. He took a chance going into the first corner when he couldn't afford to. He knew I was going to come down the inside, and he closed the door." All right-thinking people in Formula One regarded this as, at best, questionable. The telemetry system on the Honda V10 engine indicated that Ayrton had never lifted his right foot from the McLaren's throttle. It had been a deliberate strategy, and the most frightening thing about the whole episode was that Senna had been prepared to risk his life by initiating a collision with another twenty-four cars bearing down literally feet behind him.

McLaren team chief Ron Dennis joined Senna in laying much of the blame on the organizers. Senna had been trying to persuade them to move pole position back to its usual position on the left-hand side of the circuit where the line was less dirty, "Their refusal to do it created so many problems that I suppose this accident was likely to happen," said Senna, voicing a bizarre display of convoluted lateral thinking. "But that's motor racing, and the championship title is the result of a whole season's work."

At the end of 1990 Ayrton's initial three-year contract with McLaren came to an end. From then on he negotiated on an annual basis with the team, an arrangement he would continue through to the start of 1993. By then McLaren had lost its supply of Honda engines and was obliged to use Ford V8s, purchased from Cosworth Engineering on a fee-paying basis. For much of that year Senna drove on a race-to-race basis, flatly refusing to compromise on a fee requirement that would see him rewarded to the tune of $1 million every time he took his place on the starting grid.

He proved a master at turning situations to his advantage. In the middle of 1990 he began talking seriously to Frank Williams about the possibility of switching teams the following year. He opened those negotiations at a time when Honda was becoming jittery over the McLaren team's apparent mid-season slump in performance.

Honda concluded that the McLaren–Honda al-

liance had reached a critical situation and became jumpy. Senna was exerting pressure as much to maximize the terms of any future contract as to gain a competitive car, although in reality – in his mind – he wanted both.

"He is a hard and totally inflexible negotiator who will use all the methods at his disposal to maximize his position," admitted Ron Dennis. Senna eventually arranged his 1991 contract on his own terms, with both McLaren and Honda acceding to his requirements.

That season saw Honda's domination threatened quite dramatically by the burgeoning Mansell–Williams–Renault alliance, but after another mid-season technical push McLaren and Honda kept the upper hand for long enough to ensure that Ayrton was able to clinch his third Championship crown. It turned out to be his last.

The 1992 season saw Honda quite seriously off the pace. Their new V12 engine was not competitive against the Williams–Renaults, and Senna struggled to win only three races. He wound up fourth in the Drivers' Championship, which was won by Mansell, his lowest finishing position since his final season with Lotus back in 1986.

There was some doubt whether Senna would continue racing in 1993. Over the winter he stayed at home while McLaren thrashed out an engine supply deal with Ford and, even then, resolutely declined to commit himself to another season's racing with the team. Ron Dennis spent many hours, and heaven knows how many thousands of dollars, on telephone calls to Brazil, discussing, debating and analyzing the team's future prospects with the man who had become such an integral part of their operation over the past five years.

Senna's commitment behind the wheel was never in doubt.

Truth be told, Senna was irked over the fact that Alain Prost, who had taken a year's sabbatical in 1992, was now returning to lead the Williams–Renault team. Mansell had retired to the U.S. Indy-Car scene after proving unable to reach a mutually satisfactory deal for 1994 with Frank Williams, so it looked virtually certain that Alain would have a clear run to his fourth World Championship.

Senna was absolutely unyielding in his demand for $1 million per race, but Ron Dennis wanted to pay around $10 million for the sixteen-race season, obviously taking into account the fact that McLaren was now faced with the $6 million engine-supply bill from Cosworth that had not been part of the equation during that balmy five-year technical partnership with Honda.

On paper it was hard to imagine anybody but the Brazilian winning the 1994 World Championship.

season. Benetton did not win a single race until much later in the year.

For the San Marino Grand Prix at Imola, Senna only arrived at the circuit on the morning of first practice after taking an overnight flight from Brazil. A private jet was waiting at Rome airport to meet him and whisk him to Bologna and then on to the paddock by helicopter. This sort of brinkmanship was seen by some as conflicting with Senna's self-confessed professionalism. "We know that Ayrton is serious, yet a serious driver does not do things like that," said former champion Keke Rosberg. "Perhaps it was a question of business taking over from the brain."

In 1991 it was becoming clear that Nigel Mansell's Williams–Renault, seen in pursuit of Ayrton in the Italian Grand Prix at Monza, was becoming a formidable tool.

Nevertheless, Senna and McLaren inched along on a race-by-race basis, acceding to Senna's financial demands on a pro-rata basis. Ayrton was also irked by the fact that Benetton, the Ford works-backed team, also had access to higher specification V8 engines, despite the fact that he'd raced McLaren to victory in two out of the first three races that

Senna's commitment behind the wheel was not in doubt. Armed with the McLaren–Ford he added a record sixth win at Monaco to his glittering tally of success. He was able to compartmentalize his thinking in this respect. Eventually McLaren persuaded him to commit to a contract that would take them through to the end of the season together, and the team backed Ayrton to the hilt, most notably by continuing the development of its computer-controlled active suspension right through to the end of the year, even though such systems would be banned from the start of 1994. Senna's driving and the steadily increasing competitiveness of the McLaren–Ford package would help the Brazilian to round off the season with two decisive victories in the Japanese and Australian Grands Prix. But by then the romance was over.

At the Portuguese Grand Prix meeting Senna made what amounted to a coded statement to the press correctly predicting that Prost was about to announce his retirement. As a result Senna would switch to the

Dennis stated that Senna's huge financial demands had put his services beyond the reach of most teams. He also suggested that the apparent contractual deadlock, which had involved Senna competing on a race-by-race deal, was a ruse to persuade the team's sponsors to make up the difference. "I feel very sorry that Ron made these negative comments to the press," Senna reflected. "But in any case I think it will be my last season at McLaren – although not because of what has been said."

Within weeks Senna's deal with the Williams–Renault team was formally announced. On paper it was hard to imagine anybody but the Brazilian winning the 1994 World Championship. But the first

Prince Ranier (far left) looks on as Senna celebrates his 1992 Monaco Grand Prix victory in company with Nigel Mansell (right) and Jean Alesi (left).

Williams–Renault camp for 1994 in his place. He also explained that his relationship with Ron Dennis had suffered a major breach. He had been infuriated by off-the-record comments attributed to the McLaren boss in a recent briefing with British journalists that were subsequently released to *Journal do Brasil*, an influential Rio de Janeiro newspaper.

two races of the year saw Ayrton struggling harder than he had anticipated against the revitalized Benetton–Ford driven by Michael Schumacher.

Then came the third round of the title chase at Imola. The rest is shock and sadness at the passing of one of the greatest talents ever seen at the wheel of a Grand Prix car. The stark unreality lingers.

Senna conceals his disgust and disappointment – and finds time for a smile and wave to his loyal fans – after his McLaren MP4/7 suffered a failure of its Honda engine only a couple of laps into the 1992 Japanese Grand Prix at Suzuka.

Topping his own record. Senna takes the chequered flag to win the 1993 Monaco Grand Prix, setting an all-time record of six victories through the streets of the principality. With Prost retired, who will ever exceed, or even match, that record now?

(Opposite page) Waving his Brazilian national flag as usual, Senna celebrates his third World Championship after finishing second in the 1991 Japanese Grand Prix with the McLaren MP4/6. On the final corner of the race, he had relinquished the lead to his teammate Gerhard Berger in a friendly gesture to give the popular Austrian his first McLaren victory.

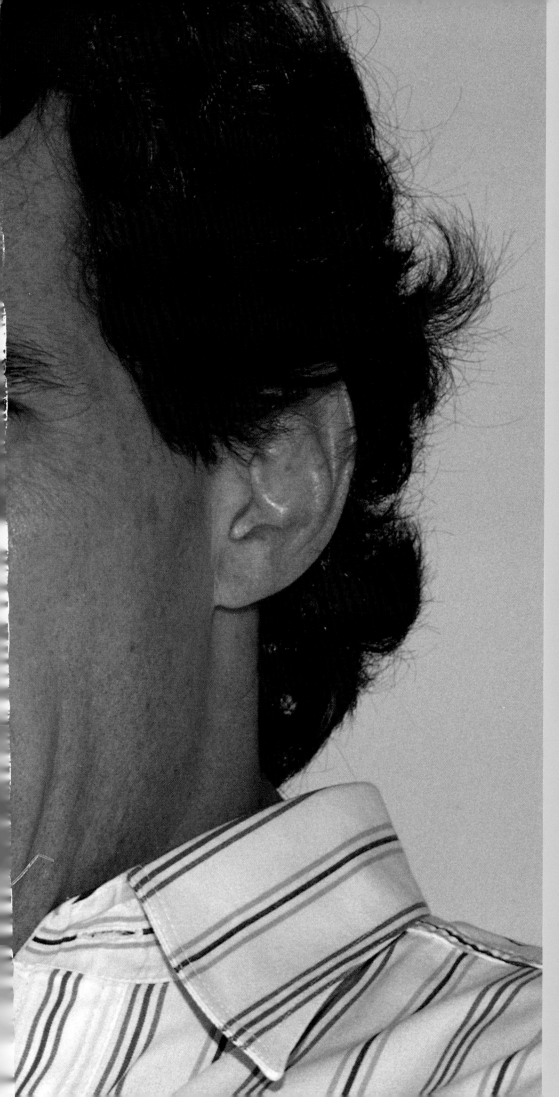

5

THE MAN BEHIND THE MASK

Generous and sensitive, ruthless and passionate, Senna encompassed a broad spectrum of human traits. He could isolate himself within a very private world, yet, paradoxically, was also concerned about his fellow men. Behind the deeply committed sportsman and business tycoon, Senna was responsible for many unrecorded gestures of philanthropy.

Apart from his quiet philanthropic activities, Senna was active with a number of business enterprises, for which his widely seen logo served as a marketing trademark. The emblem's shape was derived from a curve at Inter-lagos, São Paulo's Grand Prix circuit.

Approaching the end of the 1989 season, the paddock at the Spanish Grand Prix was swept with rumours that Ayrton Senna might retire from racing. Ironically, it was Martin Brundle who crystallized the blend of frustration and awe that the Brazilian driver engendered in his peers. "I wish he would bloody well push off back to Brazil," said Brundle half-jokingly. "It might give the rest of us a chance. There's no doubt about it, he's a great driver – damn him!" Senna had become the most respected and resented man in the business.

Admired for his towering skill, he was also disliked by many for the iconoclastic approach he brought to bear on his own personal career. He was a man who apparently conformed to none of the

the boys. For better or worse he carved a lone niche as an individualist.

Yet out on the track he displayed no such insecurities. If anything his consummate skill unleashed an overconfidence that produced as many accidents as Grand Prix victories. A rare, if uniquely flawed, talent, if you like.

For those who were involved with Ayrton Senna, professionally or personally, throughout his Grand Prix career, his death triggered a positive avalanche of memories. Everybody in the business had their own recollections of this remarkable personality. I asked him in 1988 what was the most satisfying win of a season that had seen him win his first World Championship. "It's still to come," he said after some thought.

Regal couple. With his last love, Adriene Galisteu, at Budapest's Hungaroring circuit on the occasion of the 1993 Hungarian Grand Prix.

stereotypes attached to a top-line Grand Prix driver. People did not understand his ascetic personality or the tight rein he held over his emotions.

Study all the contemporary group photographs of Grand Prix drivers taken during the second half of the 1980s and the early 1990s. Ayrton is present but seems to stand apart. He looks isolated by his own choice, perhaps not aloof, but definitely not one of

In private Senna was a man who loved his homeland with a passion. He cherished his private life, and after his early marriage failed he was seen in the company of a dazzling array of beautiful women, including Australian model Elle MacPherson. At the time of his death, his life was shared by twenty-year-old Adriene Galisteu, whom he had met in São Paulo's Limelight club on the evening after his victory in the 1993 Brazilian Grand Prix.

Friends who knew the couple well testified that Adriene had made him more relaxed and perhaps opened his awareness to the wider attractions of life outside motor racing. For the last year of his life Adriene was with Senna for much of the time, whether at his farm at Tatui, 120 kilometres from São Paulo, his home in Portugal's Algarve, or his five-bedroom mansion at Angra dos Reis on the Atlantic coast south of Rio.

Ayrton also adored his sister's children and remained reassuringly close to his own parents. Family values meant an enormous amount to this complex man, perhaps second only to his religious beliefs. You could almost feel that Senna was trying to make sense of life, to find some sort of ultimate definition, perhaps almost apprehensive that he'd been dealt such an apparently favourable hand in the material sense. He would have been a wonderful father to any child, as the manner in which he could put the most nervous youngster immediately at ease in his company surely showed.

Indeed, in the immediate aftermath of his death, it was suggested that he had a love-child who could share in his estate. Newspaper reports carried stories that Senna was the father of eight-month-old Vitoria, daughter of one-time Playboy pin-up Marcella Prad-

> *"The only motivation you can have to stimulate this passion is a desire, a determination, to first of all believe you can succeed."*

do, a model who lived in one of Rio's most fashionable suburbs.

If that was the case, then Senna's wealth certainly seemed sufficient to take care of any residual obligations. Ron Dennis may have noted that he was a hard negotiator when it came to terms for his McLaren contracts, but he was also shrewd in other areas as well. His company, Ayrton Senna Promotions, eventually grew to occupy several floors of a São Paulo office block, topped off by a helicopter pad that enabled the boss to get to work without worrying about the Brazilian city's legendary traffic snarl-ups.

Despite the slight hiccup in their relationship at the end of 1994, Ayrton Senna probably came closest to meeting his match in Ron Dennis from a commercial standpoint. Dennis, a self-made man who has steered McLaren to becoming the most successful Grand Prix team of all time, was as ferociously competitive as the man he employed for so long. Dennis wanted McLaren to win every bit as much as Senna. He admitted he felt pain when he woke up on the Monday after a race and remembered they hadn't won. He and Senna were enormously tough on each other, to the point where neither had to say a word to understand what the other was thinking.

Senna was committed to racing and winning. He didn't have time for second place and wasn't interested in mere participation. "I am programmed to win," he would say firmly. For that reason he tended to be against all the computerized control systems that gradually found their way onto Grand Prix cars in the early 1990s.

"I want to be challenged by my own limits against somebody else's limits," he explained, "by somebody who is skin and bone and where the difference is between brain and experience and adaptation to the circuit, not challenged by somebody else's computer. I don't want a car from Ron Dennis to let me win, but a car to let me compete. The regulations must be changed. The machines have taken away the character, and it's character that the sponsors and public are looking for."

Senna also found it difficult to believe that he could be wrong. After the drama of disqualification at Suzuka in 1991 he delivered the following monologue to the press immediately prior to the next race in Australia. It was riveting, uncompromising stuff offering an insight into what motivated a sportsman at the highest level.

"I think through the hard times the real personality comes out of you, and your strength becomes stronger than ever. That's the experience I have been facing for the past few days. I'm going to give my very best, despite any conditions I will give my very best because as a professional that is my duty to the team and to the sponsors of the team.

"The athlete, whether in motor racing, football or tennis – or any activity – always puts himself under a lot of stress, a lot of pressure, and leaves

Celebrating his victory in the 1990 World Championship. Ayrton's spontaneously relaxed expression betrays not a shred of guilt for the first corner collision at Suzuka in which he bundled Prost's Ferrari off the road, thereby clinching the title.

behind in life a lot of things in favour of his passion.

"You train your body to do what you want it to do, not what your body wants to do. So you put your body on the limit on many occasions, and you train your mind for the same thing – to do what you should do as a professional, as a sportsman, and not what the other man wants to do.

"The only motivation you can have to stimulate this passion is a desire, a determination, to first of all believe you can succeed. To believe you can be a winner, to believe you can compete. Once you win, what gives you the thrill, the satisfaction to motivate yourself to go through all these things, is the desire to go to the highest place on the podium.

"Therefore when anybody – at any time or any place – prevents an athlete in a competition, after

winning it, from going to the highest place on the podium, it's a major blow – to your mind, your motivations, your values, your reasons for being there. And that is what is taking place because the people who have the power have decided to do so.

"So everything goes against you, and it's only obvious that you think, 'What do I need that for?' Why should you do this, on and on, knowing that you are not being fairly treated? But, after all, racing, competing, is in my blood. It's part of me, part of my life. It's what I've been doing all my life and stands up before anything else – before any bad things can try to demotivate me.

"I know, deep inside, that the situation I have faced in the past few days only motivates me to fight against it. The reason why I'm doing that is because I

All spiffed up with the boys. Senna (left) in company with fellow World Champions (from right) James Hunt (1976), Niki Lauda (1975, 1977 and 1984) and Keke Rosberg (1982) at a bash at Monte Carlo's Sporting Club in 1992 to celebrate 20 years of Marlboro's F1 sponsorship involvement.

believe I have values which persuade me at any cost to fight to the end, so for once we can bring some justice to our sport.

"I am a professional. I have responsibilities. But I am also a human being, and the values I have in my life are stronger than many other people's desires to influence or destroy those values."

To some observers it seemed as though Senna was being pretentiously self-indulgent and delivering a monologue merely tailored for the expediency of the moment. However, the truth was that Senna was an extremely sensitive human being, even if he was sometimes hard-pressed to reflect this fact in the day-to-day Grand Prix grind.

Herein lies a baffling contradiction. This man who in his private life was generous, considerate and warm-hearted, was also the yellow-helmeted terror who almost pushed his McLaren team-mate Alain Prost into the Estoril pit wall during the 1988 Portuguese Grand Prix – deliberately, at around 175 mph.

One man who got to know Senna well, and had no axe to grind one way or the other, was Professor Sid Watkins, head of neurosurgery at the London Hospital. A passionate motor-racing fan all his life, he attends all the World Championship Grands Prix as chief of the F.I.A. Medical Commission. A straightforward man, Watkins can sniff out cant and humbug coming a mile away. It is an extremely significant index of Senna's character that the two men became close friends.

Professor Watkins, the wall of whose office at the

With Adriene Galisteu, again at Monaco's Sporting Club, during the 1993 Grand Prix weekend. Close friends hinted that she was the girl most likely to tempt Ayrton into his second marriage.

Relaxing away from the pressures of a Grand Prix weekend, Ayrton indulges his passion for radio-controlled scale-model aircraft at South Weald, Essex, during the summer of 1985.

London Hospital is dominated by a picture of Jimmy Clark in a Grand Prix Lotus, got to know Senna when he came to the medical centre at Estoril in 1984 after finishing third in that year's Portuguese Grand Prix in the Toleman. "He was very upset with the physical state in which he found himself," he recounts with an almost impish sense of fun. "He was suffering with spasms and pains in the neck and shoulders, and he didn't understand what was happening.

"In order to control the situation I issued a few short sharp words to bring him to his senses – which I cannot repeat – and then explained to him that his muscles had gone into spasm, cramp and contraction because he was short of salt. When he understood the symptoms, the first dawn of comprehension appeared in his eyes, and he became a rational person. That gleam of intellectual realization was something that would always stay in his eyes whenever he perceived that he had cracked a problem. It was a very unusual response.

"A few weeks after that he developed a facial palsy. It was just at the stage that Lotus was about to sign him, and they became very unsure about whether to proceed with the negotiation in view of this obvious paralysis and the fear it might lead to something worse. But I gave the Lotus people a lot of reassurance that his condition was localized and would not spread, because it was due to a virus infection.

"Anyway, Ayrton didn't know that was going on in the background, but he came to see me several times at the London Hospital, where he always behaved as good as gold. He turned up without pretension and without demand for recognition or rank. He sat amongst the Health Service patients and never tried to make anything out of the fact that he was an accomplished, world-famous racing driver.

"On one such occasion my secretary went down the long corridor to the waiting area and said that the next patient was Mrs Patel, an elderly Indian lady who was suffering from paralysis of the legs and was stuck in a wheelchair. Senna jumped to his feet and said, 'Can I push the wheelchair for you?' and wheeled her all the way down into my office. He said, 'Good morning, Professor," and I said, 'Good morning, Mr Senna.' He turned round, went back and sat there again as good as gold.

"This was a performance quite unlike a similar situation with another racing driver, whose name I will not mention, who turned up to be examined for re-integration after a very minor accident. He brought his manager, a PR person, a physiotherapist and BBC Television! When I'd re-integrated the young man, he turned to me and asked whether he could use my office to have a press conference. In a decent publication I cannot tell you the two words with which I disenchanted him from that view.

"Thereafter Senna and I became progressively more friendly. I admired his humility, his humour and his kindness – not on the track, perhaps, but off. And I found him a very sincere person. He would always be one of the first people to ring up if anybody was sick or injured to ask if he could help."

When racing team boss Frank Williams, for whom Ayrton would drive in his final, fateful season, was badly injured in a road accident during the spring of 1986, Senna was on the phone every day until his friend was out of danger. Even after Williams's recovery he rang, regular as clockwork, a couple of times a week for several months.

"He was a very charitable person," continues Professor Watkins, "and used his money to many good causes. The most recent one, at my instigation, provided sufficient core

> *"He always engaged his brain before his mouth – which is unusual in a racing driver, indeed in Formula One in general."*

funding for a medical service to be set up for the children of the Amazon River in the Brazilian Andes, to provide some boats, doctors and medical assistance to work in the villages. With his help it produced £250,000 guaranteed each year for five years, which is a very significant contribution. But Ayrton never wanted any publicity about anything like this.

"When he came to my home in the Scottish borders to visit and talk to the pupils Loretto school, where Jimmy Clark was educated, he asked if he could be taken to the Jim Clark Memorial Room at Duns under the condition that there was no publicity.

"At Loretto he spoke for forty-five minutes and then took questions for another forty-five minutes, from boys between eight and sixteen years old. He dealt with them beautifully, and kindly, and sincerely. Whenever he was asked a question, he would think a lot before he started to answer. He always engaged his brain before his mouth – which is unusual in a racing driver, indeed in Formula One in general.

"He was asked some very difficult questions about his religion, his relationships with other drivers and what he wanted for his future after he retired from racing, after which we went and had dinner with the headmaster. One of his other guests was the Bishop of Truro, and – typically Senna – he was soon immersed in a religious discussion, even though they were on opposite sides of the camp. Nevertheless, the Bishop thought Ayrton was a wonderful person. When he started his sermon the following day in the school chapel, he opened it by saying, 'I cannot compete with Ayrton Senna – even as a preacher.'

Ayrton loved kids and was also a shrewd business-man. He invested several million dollars creating the television cartoon character 'Senninha' in the last year of his life. It was an enormous hit with Brazil's young and was poised for export round the world at the time of his death.

aren INTERNA
GOODYEAR
Marlboro
Shell
COURTAULDS
AYRTON
Ayrton

6

AFTERWORD: WAS HE THE GREATEST?

Nuvolari? Moss? Fangio? Clark? Who was the best Grand Prix driver of all time? Senna unquestionably has a strong claim to such a distinction, but did his weaknesses preclude him from being numbered among that hallowed handful of Grand Prix legends?

(Preceding pages) Posing with a celebratory cake to record the milestone of his 50th pole position at the 1990 Spanish Grand Prix at Jerez. Ayrton always had to be the fastest, always wanted to lead, always wanted to push the hardest.

McLaren team chief Ron Dennis and Senna embrace after a victory in Japan, 1993.

Wherever motor racing fans gather, there is the inevitable debate about who was the Greatest Grand Prix Driver of all time. In many ways this is a somewhat specious debate, a bit like questioning whether a Vickers Viscount turbo prop airliner was better than Concorde.

The answer, of course, is that in comparing drivers of different generations you are comparing apples with oranges. Both are fruit, but there the similarity pretty well ends. Even so, these bar-room debates inevitably centre round the same handful of celebrated names who crop up time and time again in the contest for Pole Position in the Pantheon.

Each era has its own stars. Before the war there was the legendary Tazio Nuvolari, a frail, spindly little Italian battling the brutal, unforgiving rear-engined Auto Unions. The immediate post-war era yielded Senna's personal hero, Juan Manuel Fangio, followed by the dynamic, supremely versatile Stirling Moss and the reticent border farmer Jimmy Clark.

Later still was the calculating, intelligent Jackie Stewart, the computer-cool Niki Lauda, the immaculately neat Alain Prost and Senna himself. It's hardly worth attempting a meaningful comparison. Unquestionably, thought, they all had very distinctive qualities which set them apart from their lesser contemporaries.

Nuvolari was driven by what seemed to be a primeval urge to compete, something that sadly caused him to struggle on long past his prime. Fangio radiated an ethereal dignity that sometimes appeared at odds with his razor-sharp performance behind the wheel, while Moss was blessed with the natural energy and push that he retains to this day, even though his racing career ended thirty-two years ago and he is now in his mid-sixties.

Clark simply had genius flowing in torrents from his fingertips. He probably never wondered why he was so good, since he did not attempt any neurotic self-analysis. He just Did It. Stewart was overwhelmingly intelligent, armed with a shrewd cunning and a remarkably far-sighted disposition. Lauda could break up the business of being a Grand Prix driver into supremely logical, bite-sized chunks, and Prost applied brain power that was allied to a delicate sensitivity on his way to

winning an all-time record fifty-one Grands Prix.

Jo Ramirez, the McLaren F1 team co-ordinator, recalls meeting Senna for the first time. He was testing at Silverstone in 1981 with Emerson Fittipaldi, Brazil's senior F1 star who by then had retired to run his own rather disappointing F1 team.

"Ayrton came to talk to Emerson," he remembers, "and when he left, Emerson said to me, 'You've just met a guy who will be one of the greatest one day.' After a remark like that from him, I started to follow Ayrton's career pretty closely."

"Ayrton was born to lead, to be first, to be the fastest. That was the way he was, and it was never going to change."

Did Ramirez ever feel he got to understand what made Senna tick? "I hope I did, but sometimes I wondered," he pondered. "He was an incredibly intense person. One of his great qualities was his incredible will to win. I've never seen that sort of determination in anybody else ever. "The difference between him and Prost was that Alain, in a car he that he liked, that he was happy to drive, was

Team togetherness. Senna toasts his third World Championship and Gerhard Berger his first win at the wheel of a McLaren after the 1991 Japanese Grand Prix at Suzuka.

untouchable, unbeatable. But Ayrton at the end of the day could drive anything, no matter how badly it was handling.

"That was the case in his last race at Imola. That Williams FW16 was not a car that should have been in pole position: it was there because Ayrton was in it. Schumacher said that he could see that Senna had

(Following pages) Start of the last victory run. Ayrton's McLaren MP4/8 accelerates into the lead in the opening seconds of the 1993 Australian Grand Prix at Adelaide.

problems with the car, and anybody else might have waited a little. But Ayrton was born to lead, to be first, to be the fastest. That was just the way he was, and it was never going to change. I suppose I would have to say that you never thought [an accident] would happen to people like that – the Prosts, Stewarts, Rosbergs. They were past all that.

"Yet if it was going to happen to anybody it was probably going to happen to Ayrton, and I used to think about it because he was that sort of guy. Even if he knew the car couldn't do it, he would try to get over it. His determination was unbelievable. He would try to force the car to do more than it wanted to do." Ramirez also had glimpses of the

> *Race fans, and Senna's rivals, will argue for years over whether or not he was truly the greatest.*

overwhelmed the two men. "Just before the start of the race he called me over to do his belts up," recalls Ramirez. "I thought it was a strange thing to do as he always used to do the last pull on the belts himself, using both hands. So I came in close to the cockpit and realized he didn't want that. He said, 'It's strange for me to do this for the last time in a McLaren.' I replied, 'If it's strange for you, it is also very strange for us as well. If you win this one, I will love you forever.' Then he grabbed my arm, and I could see that there were tears in his eyes. I was actually quite worried that I had got him a little too emotional before the start."

Senna's emotional reactions in the heat of battle were also seen by many as a key shortcoming. In the 1993 British Grand Prix at Silverstone, Damon Hill's Williams got away cleanly from the start to take an immediate lead, leaving Senna's McLaren to box in Prost in third place. For the first few

Senna and Mansell were as chalk and cheese outside the cockpit of a Grand Prix car, as exemplified by this shot of the two men running wheel-to-wheel at 175 mph while battling for the lead of the 1991 Spanish Grand Prix at Barcelona.

sensitivity and emotion that Professor Watkins identified in Senna outside a pure motor-racing enivronment. One of the most intense moments in their relationship came before the start of the 1993 Australian Grand Prix at Adelaide, where Ayrton had performed sensationally in practice to put the Ford V8-engined McLaren MP4/8 on pole position.

It was Senna's final race for the McLaren team before he switched to Williams for 1994, and as Ramirez recalls, the enormity of the occasion almost

laps Ayrton drove like a man possessed, pulling all sorts of outrageous stunts in his quest to keep his rival behind.

This was irrational. There was no way in which the McLaren–Ford could compete that way, but Senna just couldn't bear to let Prost through. It was an afternoon when the Brazilian driver's innate competitiveness strayed into the realms of personal vindictiveness. Even his most ardent fans claimed he was out of order.

Champagne cocktail – home-brewed variety. Senna gives way to an untypically extroverted display with the bubbly after clinching his 1991 World Champion-ship with second place at Suzuka.

Ironically, earlier that same season Hill had pulled a similar stunt on Senna as they went into the first corner at Imola. Later the Englishman was called in front of The Master for a dressing-down. Damon just said that he'd learned all about racing tactics from Ayrton. "I don't think there was much he could say to that," recalled Hill afterwards.

At Suzuka in 1994 Senna was also badly held up behind Eddie Irvine's Jordan, the Ulsterman taking part in his very first Grand Prix and dicing with Damon Hill for sixth place. After the race he became involved in an amazing altercation with Irvine that ended with Senna striking him on the side of the face. Irvine may have been insufficiently deferential, but Senna's loss of control was yet another of those tiny glitches that emerged from time to time

when he refused to discuss the matter with the British press in Adelaide, allegedly because they had been unsympathetic in their treatment of his row with Irvine. A few years earlier, at the same race, he had lost his cool during a television interview with Jackie Stewart when the former champion suggested that he'd been involved in rather too many accidents during his career than appropriate for a man of his status.

It has also been suggested that his reluctance to test during the winter sometimes worked against him. Perhaps so, but the evidence is that he could switch himself onto a competitive pace instantly, without any need to limber up.

Jo Ramirez recalls one particular McLaren test session at Budapest's Hungaroring circuit when

Dawn of a short-lived partnership. At the start of 1994 Senna joined Britain's Damon Hill in the Roth-mans–Williams–Re nault squad. Tragedy intervened before Ayrton even got into his stride.

throughout his career to suggest that perhaps he was not, after all, the complete and rounded talent some believed. He paid for his impulsiveness when the sport's governing body punished him with a three-race suspension. Characteristically, Senna was outraged, feeling that he had been very hard done by.

His arrogance came to the surface a fortnight later

Jonathan Palmer, then the team's best driver and now part of the BBC Grand Prix television commentating team with Murray Walker, was the team's development driver. "Jonathan had covered about sixty-five laps when Ayrton arrived," says Jo, "and since he was going to take over testing the following morning, we asked if he could go out and do a lap or two just to establish whether he wanted any gear-ratio changes, or other adjustments, which we could do overnight.

"He did just a single flying lap and was two seconds quicker. Jonathan was just destroyed." It was an experience that Gerhard Berger could relate to when he first joined McLaren. While Senna spent the winter of 1989-90 resting up in Brazil, Berger submitted himself to a punishing physical regime and testing, testing, testing. He went into the new season absolutely convinced he was capable of taking on Senna in a head-to-head. But at the first race Ayrton breezed in from his holiday and took him apart.

It came as quite a shock to the pleasant Austrian, but once he came to terms with the fact that all he could do was compete for the title of 'Best of the

with him have little doubt. They were inspired and motivated by the force of his remarkable personality, his fundamentally warm disposition and his focussed energy. Perhaps the last word should go to Professor Watkins, whose observation reveals that there was still, endearingly, something of the Little Boy Lost in this Man Child who so often shielded his inner feelings from the outside world behind an seemingly granite edifice.

"Was he the greatest? I think he was the fastest, but he still lacked maturity of cunning. Despite the fact that I talked to him a thousand times about not going so fast and, instead, trying to win races at the **least** possible speed, he never took the blindest bit of notice. But on one occasion he did admit that whenever he passed my medical car out on the circuit when he

(Following page) The raw emotion of the Italian motor-racing fans –*tifosi* – is something awesome to behold. Senna is flanked by Benetton drivers Martin Brundle (left) and Michael Schumacher after winning the 1992 Italian Grand Prix at Monza in his McLaren–Honda MP4/6.

The Japanese fans loved Senna, as much for his warm public image as for his achievements in front of a succession of Honda engines. They were there to cheer him when he won the 1993 race at Suzuka, even though his McLaren by now was using Ford power.

Rest' in Senna's wheeltracks, he developed into a competitive, formidable driver. After three years alongside Senna at McLaren, Berger believed he had become a much better driver just by being close to such a genius and studying the way he operated.

Race fans, and Senna's rivals, will argue for years over whether or not he was truly the greatest. But many of the mechanics and engineers who worked

was doing something he shouldn't have been doing, he felt a bit guilty!"

Benjamin Disraeli once said of Gladstone: "He has not a single redeeming defect." Perhaps, in the end, that was the attraction of Ayrton Senna. But it was the fact that he was all too human that made his supernatural ability in racing cars so beguilingly memorable.

COMPETITION RECORD

1984
Toleman–Hart Turbo

2ND: Monaco
3RD: Great Britain, Portugal
World Championship points: 13 – 9th place

1985
Lotus–Renault Turbo

Pole positions: Portugal, San Marino, Monaco, United States East, Italy, Europe, Australia
1ST: Portugal, Belgium
2ND: Austria, Europe
3RD: Holland, Italy
World Championship points: 38 – 4th place

1986
Lotus–Renault Turbo

Pole positions: Brazil, Spain, San Marino, United States East, France, Hungary, Portugal, Mexico
1ST: Spain, United States East
2ND: Brazil, Belgium, Germany, Hungary
3RD: Monaco, Mexico
World Championship points: 55 – 4th place

1987
Lotus–Honda Turbo

Pole positions: San Marino
1ST: Monaco, United States East
2ND: San Marino, Hungary, Italy, Japan
3RD: Great Britain, Germany
World Championship points: 57 – 3rd place

1988
McLaren–Honda Turbo

Pole positions: Brazil, San Marino, Monaco, Mexico, Canada, United States East, Germany, Hungary, Belgium, Italy, Spain, Japan, Australia
1ST: San Marino, Canada, U.S. East, Great Britain, Germany, Hungary, Belgium, Japan
2ND: Mexico, France, Australia
World Championship points: 90 (94) – 1st place

1989
McLaren–Honda

Pole positions: Brazil, San Marino, Monaco, Mexico, United States, Great Britain, Germany, Belgium, Italy, Portugal, Spain, Japan, Australia
1ST: San Marino, Monaco, Mexico, Germany, Belgium, Spain
2ND: Hungary, Portugal
World Championship points: 60 – 2nd place

1990
McLaren–Honda

Pole positions: Brazil, San Marino, Monaco, Canada, Germany, Belgium, Italy, Spain, Japan, Australia
1ST: United States, Monaco, Canada, Germany, Belgium, Italy
2ND: Hungary, Portugal
3RD: Brazil, France, Great Britain
World Championship points: 78 – 1st place

1991
McLaren–Honda

Pole positions: United States, Brazil, San Marino, Monaco, Hungary, Belgium, Italy, Australia
1ST: United States, Brazil, San Marino, Monaco, Hungary, Belgium, Australia
2ND: Italy, Portugal, Japan
3RD: Mexico, France
World Championship points: 96 – 1st place

1992
McLaren–Honda

Pole positions: Canada
1ST: Monaco, Hungary, Italy
2ND: Germany
3RD: South Africa, San Marino, Portugal
World Championship points: 50 – 4th place

1993
McLaren–Ford

Pole positions: Australia
1ST: Brazil, Europe, Monaco, Japan, Australia
2ND: South Africa, Spain
World Championship points: 73 – 2nd place

1994
Williams–Renault

Pole positions: Brazil, San Marino

This edition first published in 1994 by Motorbooks
International Publishers & Wholesalers,
P.O. Box 2, 729 Prospect Avenue, Osceola, WI
54020 USA

First published in Great Britain in 1994 by
George Weidenfeld and Nicolson Ltd

Library of Congress Cataloging-in-Publication Data
is available

Printed and bound in Great Britain

PICTURE CREDITS
All photographs are © John Townsend except those
on pages 12, 13, 18, which are © Stills.